ROYAL OBSERVER CORPS

The 'Eyes and Ears' of the RAF in WW2

ROYAL OBSERVER CORPS

The 'Eyes and Ears' of the RAF in WW2

An Official History

Introduction by
John Grehan

FRONTLINE BOOKS

ROYAL OBSERVER CORPS
The 'Eyes and Ears' of the RAF in WW2

This edition published in 2017 by Frontline Books,
an imprint of Pen & Sword Books Ltd,
47 Church Street, Barnsley, S. Yorkshire, S70 2AS,

Based on file reference AIR 41/11 (entitled *The Royal Observer Corps – An RAF Narrrative*) at The National Archives, Kew, and licensed under the Open Government Licence v3.0.

Text alterations and additions © Frontline Books

ISBN: 978-1-52672-488-5

CIP data records for this title are available from the British Library

Printed and bound by TJ International Ltd, Padstow, PL28 8RW
Typeset in 10.5/13 point Palatino

For more information on our books, please email:
info@frontline-books.com,
write to us at the above address, or visit:
www.frontline-books.com

Contents

Introduction

The Silent Service

The key role played by the Royal Observer Corps in the defence of Great Britain during the Second World War has largely been overshadowed by the far-more glamourous actions of the pilots of Fighter Command and of the exciting bustle of the young WAAFs moving numbered markers around the plotting tables at the Sector Stations. Yet neither those planning nor plotting the aerial combats on the ground or those fighting the enemy in the air, could have performed with such effectiveness had it not been for the volunteers and staff of the ROC.

Though formed in 1928, at a time when the 'war to end war' was still fresh in the memory and a second world war was unimaginable to most, the embodiment of the Observer Corps, as it was then, was a highly perceptive innovation. The war of the future, if ever such a tragedy was to repeat itself after the shocking bloodbath of the Great War, would be one in which aircraft would play a major, possibly even the preponderant, role.

A system of observer posts had sprung up in the First World War which covered the Kent and Essex coasts and the London Metropolitan area – known as the Metropolitan Observation Service – and its value had been such that, with the rapidly growing speed and power of aircraft, a more extensive and well-coordinated system was considered necessary. This network was gradually expanded from London and the eastern and south-east coasts so that by the time war sadly broke out again in Europe, virtually the whole of Britain was covered, with a gap, in the main, of just ten miles between posts. It was believed in those early days that 'the bomber will always get through'. The German aircraft might, therefore, be able penetrate Britain's defences, but they would not be able to do so unobserved.

It was on Thursday, 24 August 1939, that the message went out to the volunteers of the Observer Corps to man their respective posts. War was declared just ten days later. Up and down the country thousands of ordinary people from all walks of life suddenly found their normal lives permanently disrupted. Such was their dedication that for the next five and a half years no post or centre was left unmanned.

The organisation covered 60,000 square miles with, at that time, thirty-two centres served by around 1,050 observer posts and around 30,000 observers. There were still gaps, though, in the Observer coverage, such as in north-west Scotland, west Wales and Cornwall.

Though rates of pay for these volunteers was established – the 'Class A' men undertaking to perform fifty-six hours of duty per week and the 'Class B' men agreeing to twenty-four hours' duty – some men were offended at the thought of being paid. But it was necessary to have proper written agreements that could be enforced rather than relying upon unpaid personnel.

Just how well the Observers, and the system that had been tested in trials, would perform in the heat of battle had yet to be seen. For the first few months of the war, the main enemy encountered by the Observers was boredom and the weather. But after the relative quiet of the Phoney War, the Observer Corps found itself on the front line as the Luftwaffe opened its campaign against Fighter Command in the 'Spitfire Summer' of 1940.

Whilst it was the function of the Chain Home and Chain Home Low to detect the approach of enemy aircraft, these radar systems had their limitations, in that bleeps on a screen did not indicate what type of aircraft were approaching. The other major drawback was that the radar chains were ranged around the coast and had no function inland. So, whilst the radar chains could track the enemy across the Channel, once the raiders had made landfall it was the responsibility of the Observer Corps to continue to plot the progress of the enemy aircraft as well as passing on to Fighter

Command precise numbers and types. As Air Chief Marshal Hugh Dowding made clear, 'It is important to note that at this time they [the Observer Corps] constituted the whole means of tracking the enemy raids once they had crossed the coastline.'

As the following account will reveal, the Observer Corps' reporting system was similar to, and integrated with, that of the Fighter Command, with the individual observer posts reporting into an Observer Corps Centre. The posts were manned by two people, and might be located anywhere considered suitable for aerial observation. This ranged from the tops of town buildings to sand-bagged emplacements in the open countryside.

Each area was divided into groups. Within each group there were a number of posts, which to ensure full coverage, overlapped their immediate neighbours. These were identified by a letter and a single digit. Therefore, a post might be named 'B 1' or 'C 2' and so on. There were usually between thirty and thirty-four posts in a group, each manned by around fourteen to twenty observers.

Each post consisted of a hut, in which there were a telephone, binoculars, log book, tea-making facilities and a 'pantograph' which had a height bar and sighting arm. The post also had a device for correcting height estimates which was mounted on a gridded circular map of ten miles – the ten miles that the post was responsible for.

The two observers had specific roles. When an aircraft was spotted, the observer handling the pantograph made his calculation, whilst the other man relayed the information to the group centre by direct telephone link.

A typical conversation in an Observer Post, as witnessed by one visitor went like this: 'B 3 here … the formation on 1234 are turning west – second formation on 5678 are being engaged by out fighters – my colleague says Hurricanes. Another raid of about 12, half of them two-engine bombers, are over 2345 … B3 here. That first formation now on 3456 are flying west – the 12 on 2345 have moved onto 4567 and are being attacked by a squadron of Spitfires.' As can be seen, Fighter Command was able to receive minute by minute, live information

In the Battle of Britain, the first strategic air war in history, the Observer Corps played an absolutely vital part. Throughout the four months of July to October the system had been stretched to the utmost, as day and night the plots poured in from the posts. They were then sifted and put down on a central table and, once interpreted, essential information was passed onto the RAF groups and sectors.

Just what it was like at the height of the Battle of Britain at an Observer post was experienced by a visitor to the Kent coast: 'We proceeded to the post, and after a quiet half-hour, the fun commenced. Three formations of enemy planes came in, none of them flying less than about 18,000 feet, they seemed to be composed of about one-third Dorniers and two-thirds fighters, mostly 109s. I was immediately struck with the efficient and calm way with which the developing situation was handled by the two observers on duty … At the commencement one man, with binoculars glued to his eyes, made it his job to follow closely the first two raiding formations, which were very soon attacked by our fighters. With hardly an unnecessary word gave the essential information; the man with the head phones followed the third raid and still seemed to have ears and eyes for other parts of the sky.'

The Observers became expert at their job, as testified by many in the RAF. Squadron Leader Roger Frankland, Sector Controller at RAF Biggin Hill, once stated that 'The Observer Corps were [sic] a great help. And they could sometimes give you better weather reports than the Met Office.' Likewise, Operations Room Deputy Controller Sergeant Stanley Wright declared that 'They were the fastest people I'd ever seen at recognising aeroplanes. Just give them a glimpse and they could say, "Junkers 88".'

As the Battle of Britain morphed into the Blitz, the Luftwaffe's operations became so intense that the information that poured into the Centres from the posts was overwhelming. For instance, during the attack on London on 30 December 1940, the Bromley Centre plotted 240 enemy raids in the course of just three and three quarter hours. 'At the height of the raid,' it was recorded, 'the confusion of sound was so great that it became almost impossible to separate the tracks. Furthermore, owing to cable breakages communications between posts and centre were severely dislocated. By 8.30 p.m. 33 lines were out of action. Nevertheless 160 hostile tracks were duly and correctly told to [RAF] Uxbridge and sectors.'

The heavy bombing of the Blitz inevitably meant that some of the centres and posts were hit, particularly those in urban areas. The above-mentioned Bromley Centre, for instance, was struck with incendiary bombs on the night of 16/17 April 1941. The Centre was located in a large building, Church House, which stood in a high prominent position. The roof was soon on fire and it was obvious that the old building was about to collapse; the Observers would have to evacuate. Such an eventuality had been anticipated and an emergency centre was available in a telephone exchange some 300 yards away. The men ran with their equipment to the telephone exchange and to avoid a long break in transmission during the change of location, the plotters continued to record the movements of the enemy aircraft in Church House whilst the emergency room was set up, despite blinding smoke and lumps of ceiling falling down onto the plotting table.

Coventry was the subject of frequent attention from the German bombers, with much of its city centre being reduced to rubble. The 5 Group Centre was in the middle of the city in the main automatic telephone exchange. On the night of 14/15 November 1940, some 500 tons of bombs were dropped on Coventry. Astonishingly, the telephone exchange was one of the very few in the very centre of the city that was not destroyed. The crew operating in the Centre were trapped inside the building as flames and smoke engulf the area. Telephone lines went out one by one and the lights failed. Still the men stuck to their task as best they could by candlelight throughout the night until they could be relieved the following morning. The Duty Controller, a Mr Alan Craig, was awarded the British Empire Medal.

During the Blitz, as soon as an air raid was spotted and its likely course and target estimated, sirens would sound to warn people in the likely vicinity of the attack to take shelter. Often, the enemy bombers would change direction, meaning that large numbers of people in offices in London would have left their workplaces to go to the shelters only to find that no raid had taken place in their area. This unnecessary disruption of key functions, particularly in Government establishments was costing the country dear. Winston Churchill therefore demanded the creation of a system that would produce a second warning when the attack was actually developing. The idea was that the first sounding of the air raid sirens, those people working in selected buildings would not rush to the shelters but would hold themselves in readiness. Then, if the raid became confirmed a telephone message would be sent to the buildings ordering them to be evacuated. If no phone call came, then the individuals could continue working as normal.

To help with this volunteer Observers were drawn from the Southern Area to take part in what was called the Government Subsidiary Air Raid Scheme. These men took up positions at good vantage points in London, such as on the roof of the Air Ministry or above St James' Park Underground Station. The scheme was gradually extended so that an area of 15,500 square miles was covered in which the movements of any enemy that crossed the coast between Dover and the Isle of Wight or advanced on the London area from the north between Mildenhall to Basingstoke could be tracked with precision. Eventually, this subsidiary system was responsible for more than 400 buildings, including Buckingham Palace, over an area of twelve square miles.

So successful was this scheme, it was extended across the country to include important factories where much time was being lost due to unnecessary evacuations. How this worked was detailed in a circular letter sent out in November 1940: 'That as far as possible, an "alarm" message will be sent out to selected factories and other organisations in time for 2 minutes' notice to be given to the employees of the approach of enemy aircraft; and that when the attack is over or the enemy aircraft have proceeded to such a distance that their return appears to be improbable a "release" message will be sent. This is subject to the alarm controller being satisfied that no other enemy aircraft are within 30 miles and proceeding in the general direction of the factory, etc., which has received the "alarm" message.'

The basic principle of the live minute-by-minute tracking of enemy aircraft was taken one step further to actually relay this information directly to the fighter pilots. At observer centres liaison lines were laid to Fighter Command Sector Stations and when a 'bandit' was spotted, the Observers would then give a running commentary rather than the information just being sent to Centres and then onto Fighter Command at Uxbridge and then onto the Sector Stations. This proved an immediate success, an example of this, quoted in *Attack Warning Red* by Derek Wood, concerns the night of 8/9 April 1941 as recorded in the Aberdeen Centre logbook: 'Last night we had a great success with the running commentary, and the fighter made contact in poorish moonlight and some cloud when the visibility was not more than a mile and a half and then only for silhouettes. The bandit was not definitely seen to fall into the sea but, as the pilot was exhausting his ammunition, a large portion of the [enemy] plane flew past the fighter pilot's windshield and the bandit took a lurch seawards. It was not possible to keep an accurate note of the messages sent by running commentary but two of them were as follows: "bandit on same track going east", "both planes same direction, same height, bandit just behind". This was the last message given as the fighter swung round in a short circle and immediately made contact.'

So important had the work of the Observer Corps become, it was finally given royal status in April 1941. From then onwards, the organisation was the Royal Observer Corps (ROC). Its significance was put into words by Air Vice-Marshal Ambler of Fighter Command: 'The ROC is an integral part of the command and without it the command becomes practically non-operational. The whole plotting and radar system is bound up with the ROC. One of the difficulties which will face Fighter Command is that, if the ROC is disbanded, every WAAF and airman in the command will know the command had become non-operational.'

As the war progressed, Luftwaffe intrusions became less frequent, but the Observer Posts remained manned as it could never be predicted where or when an attack would be delivered. The men had become hugely experienced and highly proficient at their jobs, so that when Hitler made his last desperate attempt at knocking Britain out of the war, it was the Observers that played a crucial role in defending the country.

It had become known in the UK that the Germans were preparing new secret weapons and from intelligence gathered from a number of sources, a fairly accurate silhouette of the V-1 Flying Bomb was prepared for distribution to Observers, along with a detailed procedure to follow if any of the new weapons were spotted. This, 'Instruction No.51 on "Diver" procedure for dealing with V.1 flying bomb attacks', was issued on 22 April 1944 – nearly two months before the first V-1 crossed the Kent coast. Understandably, it was Observers at Dymchurch on the night of 13 June 1944, who were the first people to spot the first V-1s to reach Britain.

Historian Bob Ogley described that infamous first sighting: 'Local farmer Edwin Woods was on duty on the night of June 12-13 at Observer Post Mike 3, high on the Kent Downs at Lyminge. Just after 4 am he received a message from Maidstone ROC Centre telling him there was something happening near Boulogne. Mr Wood, through his binoculars, saw a 'fighter on fire' but it was just outside his sector. He gave a reading to Maidstone and handed over to his colleagues at Observer post Mike 2 at Dymchurch.'

Mike 2, located at the top of a Martello tower on the seafront, was manned by Mr E.E. Woodland and Mr A.M. Wraight. 'At 4.08 am they spotted the approach of an object spurting red flames from its rear end and making a noise like "a Model-T-Ford going up a hill". The first flying bomb to be released against England was rattling towards them and the two spotters on top of the tower instinctively knew that the new Battle of Britain had commenced.'

It was the moment that they had been anticipating for months. For the first time the code-word for the new weapon was sounded in alarm – 'Diver, Diver, Diver'.

The men followed the strange object in the sky with their binoculars. When it had approached to within five miles of Mike 2, Mr Woodland seized the telephone and passed the warning to Maidstone ROC Centre: 'Mike 2, Diver, Diver, Diver – on four, north-west one-o-one.'

The atmosphere in the underground bunker at the HQ at Bentley Priory was relaxed that early morning. Suddenly one of the WAAF tellers sat up as if given an electric shock. She hesitated for a second, as though disbelieving what she had heard in her headphones. Then she called 'Diver, Diver, Diver' and the whole Operations Room was galvanised into a frenzy of activity: 'A dozen hands reached for telephones, the main table plotters suddenly forgot their fatigue and the controller watched in amazement as an extraordinary track progressed at great speed across the table towards London.'

The missile continued over the North Downs before it fell to earth with a loud explosion at Swanscombe, near Gravesend, at 04.18 hours. Hitler's terrifying *Vergeltungswaffe*, or 'Vengeance', campaign had begun.

It did not take long before the Observer plots of the V-1s had become highly accurate. But the speed of the new enemy machines was such that by the time the information had been passed through to the Sector Stations, there was scarcely enough time for the RAF's fighters to intercept them. So, to speed up the operation, RAF forward air controllers were placed at the Maidstone and Horsham Observer centres. With twin-channel VHF/RT radios linked directly to the Biggin Hill Sector Station, the RAF controllers were able to direct the fighters straight from the ROC plotting tables. More than 200 V-1s were destroyed in this way from the two centres.

So efficient had the ROC become by this stage of the war, it is said that not a single flying bomb to reach the UK went unobserved. When the V-2 rockets were deployed against Britain, starting on 8 September 1944, the ROC was faced with a new challenge. The ROC posts were required to give a bearing and angle on rocket trails which could be seen rising from the Continent and also to inform their respective Centres of the approximate place of impact.

In fact, the rocket trails could be spotted from remarkably far away. Sighting of rockets heading for London were often reported from the Midlands. The record is probably that of the night of 29 December 1944, when half a dozen posts to the south-east of Manchester reported seeing a V-2 which hit London around 200 miles away!

It was not just in the defence of Britain that the men and women of the ROC contributed to the defeat of the Axis. It was recognised that during Operation *Overlord* the waters of the English Channel would be filled with thousands of ships, and the skies above swarming with thousands of aircraft. In such circumstances the chances of gunners on the ships mistaking friendly aircraft for those of the enemy were clearly very high. Only one body of men had the knowledge and experience to help identify aircraft accurately – the Royal Observer Corps.

An appeal, therefore, went out for volunteers and around 1,100 men answered the call, from whom 800 were selected. Amongst those chosen was 18-year-old Graham Warner who had joined the ROC in 1943 as part of No.2 Group. He had mainly been stationed at Post H2 on Cooden Golf Course near Pevensey Bay in East Sussex. On Sunday, 14 May 1944, Graham travelled to Bournemouth where the Royal Bath Hotel had been requisitioned as a ROC training depot.

'By the very nature of things, we were a strange assortment of individuals,' Graham later wrote. 'We were all either too young, too old or unfit for military service.' Graham was in the last category and was worried that his Osteomyelitis, which had caused one leg to be turned outwards and almost an inch shorter than the other, would bar him from joining the group. However, he passed his medical examination by standing on tip-toe on his short leg, whilst praying that he would not be asked to walk.

At Bournemouth Graham and the others had two weeks intensive training, which included a 'fly-in' by captured enemy aircraft. This was described by anther ROC volunteer, J.A. Coubrough: 'On the Sunday morning, the RAF treated us to a "circus", a display of many types of aircraft we might have to identify, including three captured German machines, a Fw 190, a Ju 88 and a Me 109, each of which was flown in a group of Allied planes, with which they might easily be confused. While we lined the top of the cliff, these aircraft circled over the sea, flew along the line of the beach – sometimes so low that they were actually below us – and some of the pilots ended by coming straight in a few feet above the sea and pulling the stick back at the last possible second, so that they only just cleared our heads. It was a thrilling and, at the same time, an instructive display.'

The Air Ministry had compiled a list of the types of aircraft likely to be seen in the operational areas, and each Observer was given a set of silhouettes covering practically the whole of this list. The ROC instruction itself consisted of short talks on each of the aircraft in the list and films on the recognition features of various aircraft. They men were also shown models of the various aircraft as seen from every possible angle and under varied conditions of light.

The main focus, though, was on testing the ability of the volunteers. There were spotting tests with photographs of aircraft, a test in which the tail of one aircraft was stuck on to the body of another, with the oddest-looking results, and tests in which small models were run down wires stretched across the front of the building, while the volunteers stood on the other side of the road, trying to identify them as they flickered across white walls and black windows.

They also had to undertake what was called the 'Trade Test', which consisted of a film showing shots of thirty aircraft in flight, some fairly easy and lasting for a number of seconds, others (taken from combat films) lasting only a second in the top right-hand corner of the screen. It was a new style of test to most of the men but failure levels were surprisingly low.

After passing their tests, the men were enrolled in the Royal Navy, and given the temporary rank of DEMS PO(AI), which stood for Defensively Equipped Merchant Ships, Petty Officer (Aircraft Identifier). They were taken, 150 men at a time, to a naval school for two days. There they were taught about nautical terms, naval ranks and badges, about saluting, how to sling up a hammock and lots of useful tips, such as to wear a towel round their necks to keep them warm in the wind and to keep out rain and spray out.

The trainers also informed the observers that they did not have to actually watch for aircraft, but simply identify them when reported by the look-out men. Their task was to confirm to the gunnery officer whether they were hostile or friendly. Soon, the men were off to their respective ships with two Observers being posted to each vessel.

The system that was established, with the ROC observers controlling the gunfire of the merchant ships, worked extremely well throughout Operation *Overlord*. Indeed, it was later reported by Wing Commander P.B. Lucas, an Air Staff Officer, that: 'The general impression amongst the Spitfire wings, covering our land and naval forces over and off the beach-head, appears to be that in the majority of cases the fire has come from British Navy warships and not from the merchant ships. Indeed, I personally have yet to hear a single pilot report that a merchant vessel had opened fire on him.'

Following Operation *Overlord*, Air Chief Marshal Sir Trafford Leigh-Mallory KCB, DSO, Commander-in-Chief Allied Expeditionary Air Forces, wrote a message that was circulated to all ROC personnel and posts:

'I have read reports from both pilots and naval officers regarding the Seaborne volunteers on board merchant vessels during recent operations. All reports agree that the Seaborne volunteers have more than fulfilled their duties and have undoubtedly saved many of our aircraft from being engaged by our ships guns. I should be grateful if you would please convey to all ranks of the Royal Observer Corps, and in particular to the Seaborne observers themselves, how grateful I, and all pilots in the Allied Expeditionary Air Force, are for their assistance, which has contributed in no small measure to the safety of our own aircraft, and also to the efficient protection of the ships at sea.

'The work of the Royal Observer Corps is quite often unjustly overlooked, and receives little recognition, and I therefore wish that the service they rendered on this occasion be as widely advertised as possible, and all units of the Air Defence of Great Britain are therefore to be informed of the success of this latest venture of the Royal Observer Corps.'

Another glowing testimonial to the work of the Royal Observer Corps was given after the war: 'The general public knew nothing of the activities of the ROC and little realised that the one organisation which was in closest contact with operations of war was this pseudo-military body. In fact. the ROC was probably responsible for more damage to the enemy's war effort than most of our home-based military forces of a similar character, which must be unique in the annals of civilian national service.'

Likewise, Air Chief Marshal Sir Roderick Hill in his official report on the air defence of Great Britain during the war, wrote: 'The part played by the Royal Observer Corps – the silent service of the air defences – was an epic in itself.' What follows is an official history of that 'silent service' from 1939 until 1945.

John Grehan
Storrington
May 2017

Publisher's Note

As far as possible, this 'official history' is reproduced in the form that it was originally written. Aside from correcting obvious spelling mistakes or typographical errors, we have strived to keep our edits and alterations to the absolute minimum. A direct consequence of this policy is that there are occasional inconsistencies in the text.

Abbreviations

AA	Anti-Aircraft
ADCO	Area Deputy Commandant Operations
ADGB	Air Defence Great Britain
ADRDE	Air Defence Research and Development Establishment
AEAF	Allied Expeditionary Air Force
AM	Air Ministry
AMCO	Air Ministry Confidential Order
AMES	Air Ministry Experimental Stations
AOC-IN-C	Air Officer Commanding-in-Chief
AOGO	Assistant Observer Group Officer
ARP	Air Raid Precautions
ATC	Air Training Corps
CAS	Chief of the Air Staff
CHH	Chain Home High
CHL	Chain Home Low
Do.	Dornier
D OF I	Director of Intelligence
DDC	District Distributing Centre
DEMS	Defensively Equipped Merchant Ship
FCLO	Flying Control Liaison Officer
FGOR	Fighter Group Operations Room
FRC	Filter Room Controller
Fw.	Focke-Wulf
GCI	Ground Control Interception
GHQ	General Headquarters
GL	Gunlaying
GPO	General Post Office
HAA	Heavy Anti-Aircraft
He.	Heinkel

IFF	Identification Friend or Foe
Ju.	Junkers
LAA	Light Anti-Aircraft
LADA	London Air Defence Area
LSI (L)	Landing Ship Infantry (Large)
MAP	Ministry of Aircraft Production
Me.	Messerschmitt
MFW	Microwave Early Warning
MT	Motor Transport
OAH	Observer Area Headquarters
OAIR	Observer Area Intelligence Room
OCLO	Observer Corps Liaison Officer
OGO	Observer Group Officer
ORS	Operational Research Section
OTU	Operational Training Unit
PI	Post Instructor
PO	Procedure Order
R/T	Radio telegraphy
RAF	Royal Air Force
RDF	Radio Direction Finder
Retd.	Retired
RFC	Royal Flying Corps
RIO	Raids Intelligence Officer
RO	Routine Order(s)
ROC	Royal Observer Corps
ROCLO	Royal Observer Corps Liaison Officer
RRO	Raids Recognition Officer
SLC	Searchlight Control
SOS	International Morse code distress signal
VHF	Very High Frequency
WAAF	Women's Auxiliary Air Force
W/T	Wireless telegraphy

Chapter 1

Observer Posts in
the First World War

The story of the Royal Observer Corps would be incomplete without an account of its origin and gradual growth from the first Observer Posts in 1914 until the entry of Great Britain into the Second World War on September 3rd 1939.

The System in 1914-1915
In 1914 the defences against air attack were in the hands of the Admiralty, to whom the police sent reports by telephone of any aircraft heard or seen within 60 miles of London, and early in 1915 this system was extended to cover East Anglia, Northamptonshire, Oxfordshire, Hampshire and the Isle of Wight, and in April 1915 the War Office asked for similar messages from Chief Constables. The system was further extended to cover the whole of England and Wales, the reports to come to the Admiralty who would inform the War Office.

Warnings were issued by the Admiralty to railways and to Scotland Yard only, while interchange of information was also arranged between Chief Constables. The consequent congestion of the telephone lines can be imagined.

The War Office Takes Control
In 1916 the War Office took over control from the Admiralty, and cordons of observers were organised 30 miles outside vulnerable areas, while coastal posts were also established.

At first military personnel were used, but these proved most unsatisfactory. Many of the men were of poor intelligence and discipline was bad. This was probably due to the fact that the men employed were of necessity those unsuited for more active forms of service, and also, owing to the dispersal of observer posts, supervision was a matter of considerable difficulty.

Consequently the police were again brought in to man the posts, only two companies of the best military observers being retained to man the posts at which constant watch was required. In the autumn of 1917 Major-General E.B. Ashmore took command of the defences, and immediately realised that his biggest problem was Time-lag, a problem the importance of which increased proportionately with the speed of aircraft.

The London Air Defence Area

Early in 1918 a new system was introduced, known as the London Air Defence Area (or LADA) but, owing to the large amount of telephone construction work needed, this system was not ready for operation until after the last German raids on May 19th 1918 (see *Air Defence* by Major-General E.B. Ashmore, Chapter IV). The system worked well in practice, and the time-lag in reporting aircraft positions was found to be appreciably reduced. Under the old system, although some of the police messages were received in London in as short a time as three minutes, the average delay was much greater. Under the new system, (with its use of direct telephone lines) the time-lag was not, as a rule, more than half a minute.

As will be seen, the London Air Defence Area system may well be called, in its conception and plan, the origin of the Observer Corps organisation. It was finally put into operation on September 12th 1918.

The Lay-Out and Communications

The London area and the districts to its south and east were closely covered by the various defence units – coastal and inland watching posts, gun-stations, searchlights, aerodromes, balloon aprons, emergency landing grounds.

Each of these, now treated as an observation station was connected by telephone to a sub-control, of which there were twenty-five, each connected to two or three of these observation stations. At these sub-controls the information received of aircraft movements was plotted with counters on a large-scale map. This information was read off, by a "teller", to a "plotter" in the Central Control (at the Horse Guards) where the course was again plotted with counters on a map table.

The information was thus collected from the numerous observation centres, and passed through the sub-controls to the Central Control, where it was available for the officer in charge of defence and the Air Force Commander, who were seated in a raised gallery overlooking the map table.

The Air Force Commander could then, by means of wireless transmission, pass information and orders to his aircraft on patrol with a reasonable chance of effecting an interception.

The Reduction in Air Defences 1919-1920

From the armistice until 1920 the Air Defence quickly faded away to nothing, despite a conference at the War Office in February 1919, presided over by Mr. Winston Churchill, at which it was laid down that "the arguments for the upkeep and development of Home Air Defence were as strong as those on which the maintenance of the Navy had hitherto rested ... It was essential to keep alive the intricate and specialised art of Air Defence."

For all essential purposes, however, the London Air Defence Area may be said to have been disbanded by the end of 1920.

Chapter 2

The Reorganisation of the Observer System 1921-1928

On November 9th 1921, the standing Defence Sub-Committee of the Committee of Imperial Defence set up a special Sub-Committee "to go fully into the question of the vulnerability of the British Isles to air attack and the measures necessary to provide for meeting such attack".

A report was rendered by this Sub-Committee on April 26th 1922, with a Memorandum by the Air Staff appended to it, in which the danger and effect of an attack by the French Air Force were considered.

It will be seen that the dangers of an attack from this source were the deciding factors in the planning of the Observer Corps until the re-orientation of Air Defence was commenced in 1934.

The Sub-Committee recommended that "The organization of a zone of defence should be proceeded with", and, in this connection, suggested "that the General Staff and the Air Staff should immediately confer with a view to establishing an organization to ensure close and effective co-operation between the two services."

Joint Air Ministry and War Office Committee on Anti-Aircraft Defence

A committee was accordingly constituted under the chairmanship of Air Chief Marshal Sir Hugh Trenchard K.C.B. D.S.O., A.F.C., Chief of the Air Staff, and the first step was to set up a Joint Sub-Committee which confined its investigations to the actual defence of the area laid down for consideration, namely, "the south-east of England, south of a line drawn from Portland to the Wash". The principal members of this Sub-Committee were Air Commodore J.M. Steel and Colonel W.H. Bartholomew.

The Steel-Bartholomew Sub-Committee
The principle evolved by this Sub-Committee which deserves the greatest attention states "that a highly organised system is essential for the rapid collection and distribution of information and intelligence regarding the movements of friendly and hostile aircraft throughout the whole area of possible air operations". In the opinion of the Sub-Committee this organization was of such vital importance that they recommended its examination in detail, separately, at a later date.

In accordance with this recommendation a new joint Sub-Committee was appointed to investigate and report on the aspect of defence raised in the principle recorded by the Steel-Bartholomew Sub-Committee. The chairman was Major General C.F. Romer C.B., C.M.G., and among the members was Major General E.B. Ashmore C.B., C.M.G., M.V.O., who had taken over the defences originally in the autumn of 1917.

The Romer Sub-Committee
Among their terms of reference the Committee had "to consider and report on the system of intelligence and communication essential to the success of the Air Defence scheme and the provision of such a system". On May 16th 1924 an interim report was submitted in which it was recommended that the Army should be responsible for the provision of all apparatus and for the provision and training of the personnel required for the observation, organization and for all signal communications required by the Army, with the exception of the apparatus and personnel required for wireless communications.

The Observation System was to be organised as follows:

(i)   Sound locators, mirrors etc. were to be located at Observation Posts distributed throughout the whole of the Observation Area.
(ii)   Each Observation Post was to be in direct communication with an Observation Centre.
(iii) Each Observation Centre was to be in direct

communication with Fighting Area Headquarters; and in the case of Observation Centres adjacent to and covering Aircraft Sectors, such Observation Centres were to be in direct communication with the Headquarters of the sectors covered.

It was considered by the Sub-Committee that information obtained by Special Naval patrols, and also by certain Coastguard stations, might be of great value in amplifying the information obtained by the Observation Posts, and, in this connection, it was recommended that, when necessary, Observation Posts should be located at Coastguard stations.

The G.O.C. Ground Troops, working under the direction of the A.O.C. Fighting Area, was to be responsible during operations for the work of the observation system.

The communications necessary were considered to be a line telephone system connecting Observation Posts to Observation Centres, and Observation Centres laterally, and to Fighting Area Headquarters, and to certain Aircraft Sectors, and also connecting certain Coastguard stations to Observation Centres.

Thus the Observation System, as outlined by the Romer Sub-Committee, will be seen to be the logical amplification of the London Air Defence scheme originated by Major General Ashmore in 1918.

Sub-Committee on Air Raid Precautions, July 8th 1925
It had been agreed by the Committee of Imperial Defence on January 14th 1924, and again, after the change of Government, on February 4th 1924, that a sub-committee should be appointed to enquire into the question of air raid precautions, and that annual reports of progress should be rendered for consideration by the Committee of Imperial Defence. The chairman of this sub-committee at the date on which the first report was rendered, July 8th 1925, was the Right Hon. Sir John Anderson, G.C.B., Permanent Under-Secretary of State, Home Office. To the very thorough report submitted was appended a schedule giving particulars of the proposed warning system, and of the observation system, information supplied by this system being one of the items of intelligence on which warnings were to be issued.

In this schedule the warning system was considered from two angles, the collection of information regarding the enemy's activity, which was considered to be a service responsibility, and the distribution of that information to the threatened area. The observation system was naturally the principal factor in the collection of information, and the progress in the formation of the observation system up to that time was given in detail. Two observation zones had been organized, of which the first, with its centre in Maidstone, and consisting of 27 Posts, covered the whole of Kent, while the second, with 16 Posts and a centre in Horsham, covered East and West Sussex.

It was proposed, in the coming year, to organize observation zones in Hampshire and the Eastern Counties, and, with their completion, it was considered that the more likely lines of approach to London would be covered.

It was further proposed to give the Observer Corps a permanent standing, the members incurring no liability to carry out observation duties at a distance from their homes, the scheme depending on their living within easy reach of their Posts and Centres. With official backing, and with the members enrolled as Special Constables, it would be possible to bring the system into action at short notice, either for practice or in the event of an emergency arising.

This report was approved by the Committee of Imperial Defence on October 29th 1925.

Expansion and Exercises 1925-1928
The Observation system was accordingly extended into Essex and part of Suffolk, on the East Coast, and into Hampshire, on the South Coast, and by November 1926 four Observer Groups were established in all, the two new groups being numbered 3 and 18. Their Headquarters were at Winchester and Colchester respectively.

Annual exercises took place in 1926 and 1927, and steady progress was made in efficiency, and on March 15th 1928 the Army Council stated that they 'attach great importance to this Corps, which forms such an essential link in the ground organization of the Air Defence of London, and have followed with satisfaction the progress in organization and expansion made during the last two years'.

In the Air Defence of Great Britain Command Exercises of 1928, the Report of the Air Officer Commanding-in-Chief states that the work of the Observers improved throughout the Exercises and was excellent after the first two days. He suggested that observers should be provided with field glasses and some sound locators, and promised more practice in identification in the following year. During the night aircraft had flown over the Observer Zone with their navigation lights on, and it was proposed in the following year to extinguish these where practicable.

He was satisfied that the Corps could give good results when dealing with visible raids, but did not think that, as they were then equipped, they could give satisfactory information regarding invisible raids at a high altitude.

During these exercises an improved Observer area had been organised in the Inner Artillery Zone, consisting of eleven posts, and results had been excellent. The Air Officer Commanding-in-Chief was of the opinion that this Inner Artillery Zone should be organized as an Observer Group and that Numbers 1,2, and 18 Groups should be provided with Observer posts extending into the Outer Artillery Zone. This latter suggestion was really brought into operation some seven years later when Number 19 Group, Bromley, was formed.

Transfer of the Observer Corps from War Office to Air Ministry Control

On October 16th 1928, the Home Defence Sub-Committee of the Committee of Imperial Defence issued a memorandum recommending that the Observer Corps should be transferred from the War Office to the Air Ministry at a date convenient to the two Departments concerned.

It was pointed out that, though the "Romer" Committee had recommended that the provision and training of the personnel required for the Corps should be an Army responsibility, the Observer Corps was essentially an Air Intelligence organization. Satisfactory co-ordination between the Air Ministry and the Observer Corps could not be expected while the Air Ministry had to approach another Department in order to obtain touch with that Corps.

Four Observer Groups, extending territorially from Suffolk through the Home Counties to Hampshire had already been organized and had taken part in annual manoeuvres with promising results. There were still a further fourteen groups to be formed to complete the scheme.

A considerable stimulus was needed to develop the Observer Corps to its required strength and to maintain its interest, and it was considered that this could be best provided by the Air Ministry.

The Army Council were in agreement with the Air Council regarding this transfer, provided that the Army was relieved of all expense connected with the Corps.

This transfer was approved by the Committee of Imperial Defence at a meeting on November 8th 1928, to take effect from January 1st 1929, and a conference took place at Headquarters, Air Defence of Great Britain on November 26th 1928 to discuss details arising from the transfer.

It was decided that the four Observer Groups already formed, namely Numbers 1, 2, 3 and 18, with Headquarters at Maidstone, Horsham, Winchester and Colchester should be attached respectively to the following four Fighting Area Stations:-

Biggin Hill, Kenley, Tangmere and North Weald.

The Chief Constables of the districts concerned should be notified of the transfer and visited by representatives of the Air Force in order that details might be discussed.

Appointment of First Commandant

The Air Officer Commanding-in-Chief in a letter to the Air Ministry on November 28th 1928, stated that, in his opinion, an officer of the rank of Air Commodore or Group Captain on the retired list should be appointed as Commandant of the Observer Corps. The selection of this officer would have to be carefully made as his personality would need to be such that he could deal adequately with civilians serving in a voluntary capacity. He would carry out his duties directly under Headquarters, Air Defence of Great Britain, would be solely responsible for dealing with the Chief Constables, and would be responsible to the Air Officer Commanding-in-Chief for the training and maintenance of the Observer Posts.

A further conference was held at Air Ministry on November 29th 1928 at which the recommendations of the Air Officer Commanding-in-Chief were agreed, and it was stated that the War Office was prepared to hand over the Observer Corps as a going concern without any stores accounting transaction, the transfer including the equipment existing at centres and posts.

The appointment of the first Commandant to the Observer Corps was then made, and this position was to be filled by Air Commodore E.A.D. Masterman, C.B., C.M.G., C.B.E., A.F.C., his appointment to take effect from March 1st 1929.

Chapter 3

Development 1929-1934

On May 9th 1929 the terms of reference of the Air Officer Commanding-in-Chief, Air Defence of Great Britain, with regard to the Observer Corps, were defined by the Air Ministry. Acting through the Commandant, he was to be responsible for the administration and training, and for making arrangements for exercises. He was also to be responsible for arranging with the Chief Constables concerned the method of calling out the Observer Corps in the event of apprehended air-attack on the British Isles.

Air Vice-Marshal Ellington, the A.O.C.-in-C., thereupon recommended that a conference should be arranged between representatives of the Home Office, Air Ministry, and Headquarters, Air Defence of Great Britain to discuss arrangements for calling up the Observer Corps during the period of apprehended air attack. As he pointed out, he had little, if any, control of individual observers, and it would therefore be necessary to have them sworn in under the Chief Constables Act, 1914, and to ask them to sign an agreement expressing their willingness to be called out by the A.O.C.-in-C. He also considered that some form of emolument would be necessary for them should such a contingency arise.

Arising out of this proposal, at a conference, held on June 24th 1929, it was decided that the calling up of the Observer Corps should be left to the initiative of Air Defence Great Britain, acting through the Chief Constables, and that an approach should be made to the Home Office by the Air Ministry regarding emoluments.

Incorporation of Coastguard and Naval War Signal Stations
The Romer Committee, in 1924, had recommended that some observation posts should be located at Coastguard Stations, and this recommendation was confirmed on October 15th 1929 when it was decided that the following stations should be included in the Air Defence Intelligence System:

(a) Coastguard Stations – Orford, Walton-on-Naze, Reculvers, Kingsgate, Deal, Dymchurch, Rye Harbour, Fairlight, Bexhill, Newhaven, Worthing, and Selsey.
(b) Naval War Signal Stations:- Dungeness and Beachy Head.

Observer Posts were to be formed at each of these stations, and Chief Constables were to recruit Special Constables at each station to fill the establishment for an observer post.

These proposals were carried into effect, though the results do not appear to have been entirely satisfactory, as the personnel employed were not in all cases Special Constables, but were in some cases coastguard personnel. It was obvious that, with the limited establishment at War Signal and Coastguard stations, in some cases only 2 or 3 men, the combined duties would be too onerous. The arrangements had been that the existing personnel should be responsible for Air Defence lookout for the first twenty-four hours of an emergency and that the Observer Corps personnel should then take over the duties.

On December 8th 1930, the Admiralty, in reply to a letter from the Air Ministry, agreed that the Observer Corps should be responsible from the commencement of an emergency, through the Naval Chief Officer or Coastguard Officer would naturally remain in administrative control of the station.

Authority for Expansion Proposals Vested in A.O.C.-in-C.
In order that the Observer Corps should make steady progress in its expansion programme, the responsibility for initiating proposals regarding such expansion was vested in the Air Officer Commanding-in-Chief, Air Defence of Great Britain, the authority for this being granted on December 16th, 1929.

Formation of No.17 Group

One year later, on November 7th 1930, the Air Officer Commanding-in-Chief requested permission to form No.17 Group to cover the Hertfordshire area, with its Observer Centre at Watford. Details of expenditure, both for land line communications and for the necessary equipment for the Observer Centre, were requested by the Air Ministry. In his reply supplying these particulars, he urgently requested approval for the formation of this group. He pointed out that, since the Air Ministry had taken over control of the Corps from the War Office, no new groups had been formed, and that, besides the general benefit to training as a whole, the administrative work involved would be a valuable experience to all officers concerned in view of future expansion. Authority was finally given for the formation of No.17 Group on May 15th 1931.

It was not, however, until December 1932 that the General Post Office was instructed to proceed with the provision of the necessary land-line circuits and apparatus for the 21 posts and for the observer centre, and by April 1933 the group was at last formed, two and a half years from the date of the original request by the Air Officer Commanding-in-Chief.

Joint Chief Constables' District Conferences 1929 and 1930

On October 22nd 1929 a conference was held at which were present Chief Constables from No.5 and 6 Districts (comprising all the area to be covered by Observer Posts as then planned), at which the chairman was Mr. A.L. Dixon C.B., C.B.E., of the Home Office. The progress of the Corps was reviewed by the Commandant and its system of operation was explained. The Chief Constables were also informed that the air raid warning system was based on information supplied by the Observer Corps. Very careful organisation and training were therefore necessary, not only for the sake of active operations against the enemy, but also to safeguard the civil population.

Air Commodore Masterman, the Commandant, said that the work of the Corps during the summer exercises of 1929 had been very satisfactory, but that, during the coming year, the exercises were to be more concentrated, and a greater density of aircraft provided, and thus there would be a closer test of work at the Observer Centres.

On December 3rd 1930, The Chief Constables of the same districts again met so that the Commandant of the Observer Corps might deal with any points that had arisen during the past year. He dealt with various matters concerning the arrangements at the Centres and the manning problem, asking Chief Constables to endeavour to reach the total strength of sixty men for each Centre. The Chief Constable of Colchester, at which centre the position was particularly unsatisfactory, was unenthusiastic about the Observer Corps as at present organized and gave it as his opinion that it should be on a fulltime basis as an auxiliary part of the Air Defence System. He was doubtful of the practical value of the Corps, and considered that the position would become worse with the development of aircraft. He doubted, particularly, the power of an observer to detect fast flying aircraft at great height by night.

The Commandant anticipated that night bombers would be slower and would fly at lower heights. He considered that the last exercises showed that further training was necessary in detecting fast machines during the day, but pointed out that this was the first occasion when posts had been required to report all aircraft seen, and not merely bombers, and that there had been at least twice as many aircraft in the air as there had been in previous exercises.

The question of height-finding was raised, and it was explained that the function of coastal posts was principally to supply an approximate indication of the position of the aircraft to assist the adjacent posts to gauge the height by cross-observations.

Appointment of an Assistant Commandant
In 1931, it was found that the work involved in the individual inspection of each of the 4 centres and the 118 posts, performed of necessity during the 9-10 weeks of the exercise periods, was too great to be carried out by the Commandant alone. It was, therefore, recommended that an Assistant should be provided. This request was rejected by the Air Ministry on the grounds of the existing financial position, but on the proposal being again

put forward the following year, financial approval was given on February 1st 1933.

As a result of this Group Captain I.T. Courtney C.B.E. (Retired) was appointed Assistant Commandant, his appointment to take effect on March 1st 1933.

Formation of No.16 Group

By October 1933 the Observer System comprised five completed groups Nos. 1, 2, 3, 17, and 18, and covered the Coastal area from Suffolk to Hampshire and the inland area extending into Berkshire, Buckinghamshire and Middlesex. The next area to be covered in logical sequence was the northern portion of Suffolk and Norfolk. Accordingly, on October 18th 1933 the Air Officer Commanding-in-Chief requested permission from the Air Ministry to proceed with the formation of this group. At the same time he mentioned that the succeeding group to be formed would be No.4 Group, at that time intending to cover the county of Dorset.

It is at this period that indication is first given that the situation in Europe was changing, for with the growth of the German Air Force a possible re-orientation of the Air Defence System of Great Britain was being considered. Instructions were given that the formation of No. 4 Group was to be postponed as it was considered that it might prove advisable to site the next Observer Group further to the North.

In the meantime the formation of No.16 Group was commenced, 27 Observer posts were selected, and the General Post Office were asked to make arrangements for the provision of the necessary circuits and equipment.

Sub-Committee on the Re-orientation of the Air Defence System of Great Britain

In the light of Germany's re-armament in the air and the consequent changes in the situation, the Home Defence Committee appointed a Sub-Committee to consider the Re-orientation of the Air Defence System of Great Britain. This was under the Chairmanship of Air Chief Marshal Sir Robert Brooke-Popham, K.C.B., C.M.G., D.S.O., A.F.C., Air Officer Commanding-in-Chief.

The original air defence scheme founded on the "Steel-Bartholomew" and "Romer" Reports had attempted to provide against possible air attacks from French territory, and, with the then limited range of aircraft, it had been considered sufficient to confine the defence system to that part of England south-east of a line drawn from the Wash to the Bristol Channel. It was now necessary to provide against attack on Northern England and the Midlands.

Among the general principles on which the deliberations of this Sub-Committee were based was the following:- 'that a highly-organised intelligence system is essential for the rapid collection and distribution of information regarding the movements of friendly and hostile aircraft throughout the whole area of possible air operations'.

It was recommended that the Observer Corps organization should be expanded to cover the whole of that part of England enclosed by the East Coast up to Middlesborough, a line drawn thence to Preston, thence roughly parallel but to the east of the boundary of Wales as far as the South Coast, and thence along the South Coast in an easterly direction.

This expansion, which would now cover the whole of England, with the exception of the extreme North and the South-west, would obviously involve considerable increases in the organization and training requirements of the Observer Corps. A further Sub-Committee was therefore appointed to examine and report upon the details of the organization required. Air Commodore O.T. Boyd, O.B.E., M.C., A.F.C. was appointed as chairman.

After two meetings in December 1934, the report of this Sub-Committee was finally produced on January 17th 1935.

Chapter 4

Reorganization and Development 1935-1939

Broadly speaking, the Boyd Sub-Committee were required to report upon the measures necessary to expand the observer organization to cover, by 1939, an area of England lying south and east of the line Middlesbrough – Preston – Mersey – Crewe – Worcester – Cheltenham – N.E. of Salisbury – Poole.

In studying this problem it was necessary to investigate the organization and personnel required for the training and technical administration of the expanded Observer Corps, bearing in mind that, at that time, six Observer Groups were being controlled by a Commandant and an Assistant Commandant only.

In the Terms of Reference it was stated that it was necessary 'to investigate whether any change in the conditions of enlistment of personnel of the Observer Corps is desirable in order:

(i)   to facilitate the recruitment of personnel for training in time of peace;
(ii)   to ensure the effective working of the Observer Corps during the early period of war;
(iii) to facilitate the formation of an overseas contingent.'

Working on the assumption that an efficient Observer Corps was the basis of the Home Defence intelligence organization, it was recommended that an increase in full-time paid officials was necessary for Command and administrative duties. It was considered desirable that the officials who were ultimately to be responsible for this training and administration should be those entrusted with the task of forming the new Groups. With regard to the Group boundaries, while it was preferable that these should conform to those of the counties, it might be necessary to define them arbitrarily, as the limiting factor must be the need for the map table at each Observer Centre to be of convenient size and shape for plotting the information received from the Posts.

It was recommended that the Observer Corps organization should be divided into two Areas, Southern and Northern, whose communications organization must be suitably adapted to the two Fighting Area Commands, while Observer Centres near the junction of the two Commands would report direct to both the Fighting Area Headquarters. The question of communications would be referred to the Home Defence Land-Line Telephone Committee when the organization of the Home Defence System was decided.

The Southern Area was to comprise Nos. 1, 2, 3, 4, 12, 15, 16, 17 and 18 Observer Groups, and the Northern Area Nos. 5, 6, 7, 8, 9, 10 and 11 Groups. Thus the system was to consist of sixteen Observer Groups instead of the eighteen recommended by the Romer Committee in 1924.

The full-time paid officials necessary for Command and administration duties were five in number, a Commandant Observer Corps, a Southern Area Commandant and a Deputy Commandant, a Northern Area Commandant and a Deputy Commandant.

In addition to these full-time officials there should be Observer Group Assistants, each of whom was to be responsible for the administration and training of the observer posts in his group. These officials should be recruited as part-time officials for six months duty each year, from March 1st to September 1st, and should be paid a retaining fee for their services.

A development table was prepared showing in detail the stage of progress to be reached on March 1st of each year, the final organization to be completed by March 1st 1939. In order that officials should be fully trained by the dates on which they had to assume responsibilities in connection with the formation of their own particular Areas and Groups, it was strongly recommended that they should be attached to other Groups during the preceding year so that they might study the process of raising and organising new groups and the training of existing groups.

The Sub-Committee recommended that a conference of Chief Constables should be called, when their report was approved, in order that the Commandant might explain the revised organization, and take the Chief Constables into consultation with a view to ensuring that the right type of man was available for the appointments of Observer Group Assistants.

It was considered that the position of observer on the outbreak of war needed to be more clearly defined, in view of the importance of an efficient observer organization being available during the early phase. They therefore recommend that, dating from the day on which he was called out in connection with a national emergency, no member of the Observer Corps should be removed compulsorily from his duties in connection with the emergency during the first month, nor should he be permitted to resign from the Observer Corps within the first week of such an emergency.

It was anticipated that no difficulty would arise in raising an adequate number of volunteers for service overseas should such a necessity arise. It was not, however, considered politic to make public at that time any suggestion that such a contingency might arise. It might affect recruiting, conveying, as it would, the false impression that an offensive policy was to be pursued.

Approval by Home Defence Committee and by the Committee of Imperial Defence
In January 1935 the Boyd Sub-Committee submitted its report to the Sub-Committee on the Reorientation of the Air Defence System of Great Britain. In his covering note to the Home Defence Committee, Air Chief Marshal Sir Robert Brooke-Popham, the chairman, approving the Report, made the following comments:

(i) That before the end of the five-year period, finishing in 1939, it would probably be necessary to consider the question of a further expansion of the Observer Corps, both in the light of anticipated aircraft development and in the light of improvement in methods of detection developed by research.

(ii)   It was not anticipated that the total was strength of the Observer Corps, approximately 6,000 on completion of the proposed scheme, would materially affect recruiting for the Territorial Army, as normally the personnel for the Observer Corps would be either under twenty or over forty-five years of age.

(iii) It was recommended that the Air Ministry should give close attention to the matter of the provision of aircraft co-operation in the training of the Observer Corps.

The Home Defence Committee approved the Report and endorsed the Chairman's covering note on April 11th 1935. The Committee considered that a constant review of the rate of progress of the expansion of the Observer Corps should be maintained. It was recommended that the Committee of Imperial Defence should approve the proposals contained in the Report and the Chairman's covering note.

On April 16th 1935 the Committee of Imperial Defence considered the report and approved it subject to the necessary financial arrangements being settled between the Treasury and the Air Ministry.

Chief Constables' Conference, April 1935

In compliance with the suggestion made by the Boyd Sub-Committee, a conference of those Chief Constables whose districts were concerned in the reorganization of the Observer Corps was held on April 17th 1935. The Commandant explained to the Chief Constables the proposals put forward in the report, and the decisions regarding personnel. After discussion, it was decided that the Chief Constables concerned in each of the Observer Groups 1, 2, 3, 16, 17 and 18 should submit names of likely candidates for Observer Group Assistants to the Commandant, who would make the final selection.

The Commandant stated that he proposed to carry out a survey in the autumn of 1935 to decide the siting of Observer Groups 4, 12, and 15, and asked the Chief Constables in the area concerned to recruit personnel for the Observer posts on the basis of 6 observers for each post in the first year and 12 in the second.

Calling Out the Observer Corps

In May 1935 it was realised that it was necessary to come to some standardised system for calling out the Corps in an emergency, and, in this connection, a memorandum was circulated from the Home Office for consideration, and a conference was held on June 6th 1935 at the Home Office on Air Raid Warning Districts and the Observer Corps.

General agreement was reached on the desirability of a full exercise of lighting restrictions and air raid warnings in conjunction with the Air Defence of Great Britain exercise of 1935, but it was pointed out that this exercise could only take place within the area covered by the Observer Corps. This point led to a discussion on the subject of the Observer Corps expansion programme generally and its relation to the Air Raid Warning System. It was realised that without an observer system it was impossible to operate any warning system, and it seemed, therefore, essential either that the Air Ministry should say publicly that certain parts of the country could be safely regarded as immune from liability to attack from the air, or that some observer system should be provided for the whole country. It was possible that observer posts could be more widely spaced in certain remote areas. It was agreed that this matter should be raised with the Home Office Defence Committee. The conclusions reached regarding the calling out of the Observer Corps were as follows:

(1) That there should be three stages – 'Readiness', 'Alert' and 'Released'.

(2) 'Readiness' would mean the full manning of all posts and centres, with the men at the posts actually on the lookout with their instruments. Telephone connections would be made and tested and all other steps taken to ensure that the Observer Corps could operate on a war footing.

(3) 'Alert' stage should be such that 'Readiness' could be reached in five minutes. At this stage two men would still be needed at each post, but they could be resting and within call of the telephone from the centre. At the centre, half the crew should be on duty, the other half being allowed to go home, subject to recall at any time.

(4)   'Released' would mean that all men could be relieved from duty, and conditions must be such that 'Readiness' stage could be attained within two hours.

As has been seen, it was beginning to become obvious that the expansion of the Observer Corps, as at present planned, was not likely to be of a sufficient extent to meet the demands for annual exercises, let alone those of war. This opinion was expressed, and suggested matters for further discussion were raised, in a memorandum issued by the Home Office on August 1st 1935.

It was pointed out that the following areas would not be covered by any observer organisation under the present scheme:

(i)   Bristol and the Western Counties.
(ii)   The whole of Wales, together with the English Counties between Birmingham and Wales, and
(iii) The country north of a line from the Tees to the Ribble.

Thus, if raiders crossed the coast west or north of the Observer area, or passed through Observer area and beyond it, there would be no machinery for keeping track of their further movements, and air raid warning could not be issued with any pretence of accuracy. The approach which was, at that time, being made to local authorities on the subject of air raid precautions must be made on the assumption that it was possible to send air raid warnings to all the districts concerned, an assumption which could not be substantiated under the conditions then existing.

The following points, therefore, required further consideration and discussion:

(i)   The ratio of expansion of the Observer Corps within the present plan.
(ii)   Provision for reporting hostile aircraft outside the area at present planned to be covered by the Observer Corps.

Passive and Active Defence
These points were the basis of considerable inter-departmental discussion and correspondence during the ensuing months, in particular between the Home Office and the Air Ministry. In the

opinion of the Home Office the extension of the Observer system was to be regarded as an urgent matter, and it was also necessary to accelerate the completion of the organization as then planned.

This view, in their opinion, took into account the claims both of passive and of active defence. From the viewpoint of passive defence it was essential, in the interest of security, the air raid warnings could be provided in every part of the country, while from the aspect of active defence, in order to be able to effect interception of hostile aircraft, it was essential to provide continuous tracks of their progress.

This view was strengthened by the opinion expressed by the Scottish Office, which considered that 'it would be difficult to justify the absence of a warning system for any part of the country', and that there could be no such warning system in those parts of the country not covered by the Observer Corps. It was accepted, however, as a convenient preliminary stage, that the planning of the system should, for the present, cover only the South and East of Scotland up to a line from the mouth of the Clyde to Aberdeen.

The Air Officer Commanding-in-Chief was requested to forward his views on the practicability of completing the expansion scheme for the Observer Corps at a date earlier than that contemplated by the Boyd Committee report, the date suggested to be either March 31st 1937 or, alternatively, March 31st 1938.

In his reply he pointed out that the expansion was, of necessity, closely related to the expansion of the Royal Air Force, in that, when an Observer Group was formed, it required an R.A.F. organization to which it could report, and also aircraft conveniently situated for exercise purposes. The formation of an Observer Group before it could function in relation to its appropriate sectors would be harmful to the personnel.

Assuming that these requirements were met, that the additional staff required could be obtained, and that the General Post Office authorities could provide the necessary communications, the expansion could be completed by either of the dates mentioned.

At a conference held on July 3rd 1936 between representatives of the Air Ministry, the Air Raid Precautions Department and the

General Post Office, the extension of the Air Intelligence System was discussed in its relation to the provision of Air Raid Warnings in the light of the increased speed and range of aircraft.

It was recognised that the present Observer system contained no provision north of the Tees, and, acting on the principle that a belt of coastal observer zones provided cover for the belt behind, it was agreed that it would be sufficient as a first step to provide additional Observer Groups from the Tees up to, and including, the Firth of Tay, thus covering the Clyde and, to some extent, Barrow and West Cumberland.

The conclusions reached at this conference were as follows:

(a) That the suggested extension of the Observer System beyond the area at present planned might be left in abeyance, subject to the minor extension referred to in (c).

(b) That the formation of number 9 Group (North Yorkshire) should, if possible, be accelerated to be completed by March 1937.

(c) That additional Observer Groups (Numbers 30 and 31) were desirable along the coastal belt from Number 9 Group to the Tay inclusive, these Groups also to be formed, if possible, by March 1937.

Thus, with the completion of Numbers 10 and 11 Groups, covering the East Riding of Yorkshire and Lincolnshire, by March 1937, as planned, the coastal area of England and Scotland would be covered from Poole to the Firth of Tay by that date.

Formation of Numbers 4, 12, 15 Groups

By October 1935 the three groups, scheduled by the Boyd Committee to be completed by March 1st 1936, were in process of formation. These were Observer Groups Number 4 (Oxford), 12 (Bedford), and 15 (Cambridge). Numbers 4 and 12 Groups were to have 18 posts each, and Number 15 Group 21 posts.

The formation of these three groups together with their staffs, would complete the whole of the Southern Area of the Observer Corps, and the way would then lie clear for the formation of the Northern Area, commencing on March 1st 1936, with Number 10 Group (York) and Number 11 Group (Lincoln).

The Northern Area, Observer Corps

On May 13th 1935, Group Captain V.O. Rees was appointed Commandant of the Northern Area of the Observer Corps. Permission was requested by the Air Officer Commanding-in-Chief to acquire temporary accommodation for a Northern Area Headquarters at Doncaster, though it was assumed that the Headquarters would eventually be established in or near York, depending on the location of Headquarters of Number 13 Fighter Group.

Change of Commandant, Observer Corps

Air Commodore E.A. Masterman, who had held the position of Commandant since 1929, retired on March 1st 1936, and his place was taken by Air Commodore A.D. Warrington-Morris C.M.G., O.B.E.

Formation of Numbers 9, 30 and 31 Groups

As a result of the Inter-Departmental conference held in July 1936, the Air Officer Commanding-in-Chief was asked for his opinion as to the effective dates of completion of Number 9 Group and of the two proposed new Groups. In his opinion, provided instructions to proceed were given by September 1st 1936 in the case of Number 9 Group, completion could be by the end of March 1937; in the case of the two new Groups (subsequently numbered 30 and 31), if orders to proceed were given by October 1st 1936, completion could be by May 31st 1937. The completion of these Groups would have no effect on the date of completion of the remaining Groups which had already been approved.

Instructions to proceed were finally received on November 1st 1936, and it was decided that the Observer Centre for Number 30 Group should be at Durham, and for Number 31 Group at Dunfermline.

The "Ideal" Air Defence of Great Britain

In the meantime, the growing strength of the German first-line bomber strength, and the consequent necessity of making provision for the protection of vital points and for warning the civil population of impending air attacks had revived the whole question of the scale of anti-aircraft defence.

A sub-committee of the Home Defence Committee, under the chairmanship of Air Chief Marshal Sir Hugh Dowding K.C.B., C.M.G., was appointed to consider the requirements of an "Ideal" Air Defence of Great Britain, and on this committee were representatives of all the Services. Among the Terms of Reference was the recommendation that they should review the approved scheme for anti-aircraft defence, including the provision of fighter aircraft, and the plans for anti-aircraft defence of posts, and make recommendations as soon as possible as to the "ideal" defence they considered desirable, irrespective of considerations of supply.

In their report, submitted on February 9th 1937, they considered that, in view of the increase in bomber ranges, a measure of protection must be provided for the Tyne-Newcastle, Forth and Clyde, and Bristol areas. They recommended that aircraft sectors should be formed, in addition to those already approved, to guard these and other areas.

As an extension of the Observer Corps System for the defence of South East Scotland had already, in part, been implemented by the commencement of the formation of Numbers 30 and 31 Observer Groups, it was recommended that a further extension should be approved to cover the Bristol and the Clyde areas.

These recommendations were incorporated in a Joint Air Ministry and Home Office Note for which the approval of the Committee of Imperial Defence was requested on July 22nd 1937 in a Memorandum by the Home Defence Sub-Committee, in which they stated that 'it would not be justifiable to delay the adoption of measures on which the Home Office warning arrangements are entirely dependent'.

Approval was given by the Committee of Imperial Defence on July 29th 1937, and it is as well to give this proposed expansion in some detail inasmuch as it was the completion of the Observer Corps, with the exception of various minor alterations and amendments, to its state at the outbreak of the Second Word War.

It was premised that the obligation of the Home Office to provide adequate warning of the approach of hostile aircraft could only be fulfilled if constant track were kept of the movements of all such aircraft whilst over this country. A properly organized system was therefore necessary whereby reports of such movements could be passed to one or more central headquarters.

The increase in the range of bomber aircraft had brought all England and Scotland within the area of possible air attack. It was not, however, considered necessary at that stage to set up an organized system of observers in Northern and Western Scotland, Western Wales, or Cornwall. This would only become necessary when the approach of hostile aircraft via the western seaboard became a serious possibility.

Central Scotland – Active Defence
In addition to the formation of Numbers 30 and 31 Groups, whose completion was now expected by June 1938, it was considered that the air defence of Central Scotland required the formation of three additional full-scale Observer Groups. These Groups, numbered 34, 35 and 36, extended south to the Lowther Hills and included Stirling, Glasgow and Perth.

Remainder of England and Scotland – Passive Defence
The remaining area of England and Scotland required cover for warning purposes, but lay too far to the west and north to be of any direct value to the active defence system. It was therefore proposed to cover this area with fourteen groups on a less highly organized scale. Nine of these groups, numbered consecutively from 21 to 29, extended from Devon and Dorset north to Cumberland and Westmoreland. Number 32 Group covered Eskdale and the Scottish Border. Numbers 37 and 38 Groups continued the coastal cover northwards through Forfar, Aberdeen and Elgin. The necessity for the remaining two Groups, Numbers 33 and 39, was considered doubtful at that time, and it was proposed that the question of their formation should be reviewed in twelve months' time. Number 33 Group covered the Wigtown peninsula and Kircudbrightshire, while Number 39 Group was centred round Inverness.

Although it was solely to meet Home Office needs that the fourteen groups were to be organised it would make for greater efficiency and economy of staff if they were supervised and administered by the Air Ministry. This would also facilitate their development to a full-scale observer organization if enemy activity and the air defence system necessitated that change.

As it was considered that the Home Office should be in a position to fulfil their warning obligations as soon as possible, it was desirable that the expanded system should be in operation by 1939.

Views of the Air Officer Commanding-in-Chief

In reply to a request from the Air Ministry, the Air Officer Commanding-in-Chief, on April 2nd 1937, made various comments and suggestions on both this scheme and on the Boyd Committee scheme for Observer Corps expansion. He mentioned an additional Group (Number 19 with centre at Bromley) which had been authorised to cover the approaches to London form the immediate North, East and South. He proposed that this Group should be formed by June 30th 1938 (the plotting in this zone (the Aircraft Flying Zone) had been performed hitherto by searchlight personnel of the Territorial Army).

He pointed out that the date of March 31st which had been given as a standard annual time for completion of the formation of Observer Groups, was unsatisfactory as training could not be given during the winter months without serious difficulty. He recommended that June 30th should be taken as the standard date in future. Owing to the fact that there was no Fighter Group Headquarters at that time in the West of England he suggested that an Observer Area Intelligence Room should be formed at either Bristol or Gloucester (the latter was chosen subsequently) to which Numbers 21 and 27 Centres should report.

He proposed various accelerated dates for the formation of the remaining groups, but these dates proved not to be practicable owing to the time taken for these proposals to be approved.

On August 14th 1937, the Air Ministry notified the Air Officer Commanding-in-Chief that his suggestions were approved, and that he was to implement this decision as soon as practicable.

The latter thereupon submitted the following revised proposals for the formation of Observer Groups:

1937-1938 Complete Numbers 7, 8, 19, 23, 24, 30 and 31.
Survey Numbers 5, 6
1938-1939 Complete Numbers 5, 6, 22, 25, 27, 29, 34 and 35

1939-1940 Complete Numbers 21, 26, 32, 36 and 37
1940-1941 Complete Number 38

After discussion with the traffic department of the G.P.O., it had been decided to cancel Number 28 Group, and to absorb the area concerned into Numbers 29 and 32 Groups.

The Air Officer Commanding-in-Chief also suggested locations for the various Observer Area Headquarters – Scottish at Edinburgh, Northern at Catterick, Midland at Hucknall, Southern at Bentley Priory, Western at Gloucester.

These suggestions were approved by the Air Ministry on September 15th 1937.

Formation of Nos. 5, 6 and 14 Groups

During 1938, the expansion, recruiting and training continued at maximum speed, and by May 31st the progress made in the formation of Observer Groups Number 5 (Coventry) and Number 6 (Derby) had been so rapid that it was found possible to advance the date of completion to September of that year instead of June 1939, approval for this being given by the Air Ministry. Experience showed, during the exercises of 1938, that there were insufficient observer posts in Norfolk, Suffolk, and Essex to provide continuous and satisfactory tracking of aircraft. As the addition of the necessary posts to the existing groups would have rendered Numbers 16 and 18 Groups unwieldy, a new group, Number 14, was planned, and it was decided that the centre for this should be at Bury St. Edmunds.

The Crisis of 1938

The first full scale call-out of the Observer Corps took place on September 26th 1938, when the strained relationship with Germany brought on a state of crisis. The call-out was satisfactorily completed, centres and posts being manned at 1800 hours on that date, and most of the telephone lines being through by the time stated. Subsequently, crews were dismissed with orders to report for duty at certain specified times to receive further instructions. This arrangement continued in force until October 1st, when crews were finally dismissed, and Observer Corps lines were restored to public service.

Prior to the actual call-out, all Area Commandants had been supplied with drawings of a standard pattern hut for posts, together with the necessary official documents to landlords and tenants regarding their erection at post sites. Many of the huts were erected by local labour within a few days of the emergency arising.

Allocation of Groups to Areas
From October 1938 until August of the following year formation of observer groups continued steadily, it being laid down on September 24th 1938 that, as from October 10th, the allocation of groups to Areas was to be constituted as follows:

Southern Area:- Numbers 1, 2, 3, 4, 17, 18 and 19 Groups
Midland Area:- Numbers 5, 6, 11, 12, 15 and 16 Groups
Northern Area:- Numbers 7, 8, 9, 10 and 30 Groups.

Formation of Further Groups
From this date it was becoming increasingly obvious that war was inevitable, so much so that on March 29th 1939 it was stated that 'in view of the present international situation the Air Ministry are reluctant to consider any plan for forming 14 (Bury St. Edmunds) Group which involves closing down Numbers 16 and 18 Groups for a period of 11 days' (which had been the period considered necessary by Headquarters, Fighter Command). It was suggested by the Director of Operations that a new plan should be drawn up for the formation of this group which ensured the maintenance of an Observer Corps service on a reduced scale in the areas then covered by Number 16 (Norwich) and Number 18 (Colchester) Groups.

In the meantime the formation of Scottish Groups was proceeding rapidly, Number 31 Group (Galashiels) and Number 36 Group (Dunfermline) being formed on May 9th 1939, Number 34 Group (Glasgow) on June 6th 1939, and Numbers 32 Group (Carlisle), 37 Group (Dundee), and 38 Group (Aberdeen) all being in process of formation, with the expectation of completion by the end of 1939.

In England, Number 29 Group (Lancaster) was formed on June 2nd 1939, Number 26 Group (Wrexham) on July 15th, and the

Number 14 Group (Bury St. Edmunds) was completed on June 24th 1939.

Thus the whole of the Southern Area (Headquarters Stanmore), the Northern Area (Headquarters Catterick), and the Midland Area (Headquarters Grantham), in which latter had been included Number 14 (Bury St. Edmunds), had been completed by the exercises of 1939, as had also parts of the Western Area (Headquarters Gloucester) and the Scottish Area (Headquarters Edinburgh).

At this point it may be as well to mention that the three groups mentioned above, whose formation was expected by the end of 1939, namely Groups Number 32, 37 and 38 were, in fact, completed by December 20th, October 18th and November 1st 1939 respectively.

Exercises – August 1939
It was arranged that a three day full scale exercise of the defences should take place from August 9th to August 11th 1939, in which the following organizations were to participate:

56 Bomber Squadrons, 31 Fighter Squadrons,
4 Anti-Aircraft Divisions, the Observer Corps and the
Air Raid Warning Organization.

The object of this was to provide practice for all these formations in conditions approximating as nearly as possible to those of war time. Certain of the Bomber Squadrons represented friendly aircraft while others represented hostile. All squadrons were assumed to be friendly when flying out to the North Sea, the 'friendly' squadrons turning back at the coast while the 'hostile' proceeded further out to sea before turning.

In these exercises there was a considerable amount of low cloud and a good deal of plotting was therefore by "sound" and this, of course, presented a difficult task for observers.

During this exercise the Radar system was in operation, and to the Filter Room at Headquarters Fighter Command were passed plots of aircraft or formations of aircraft picked up and tracked by Radar Stations. In this Filter Room 'Tellers' placed so as to overlook the map table 'told' forward the incoming plots to the

Fighter Command Operations Rooms. This information was then "retold" to the Coastal Observer Centres by "sea-tellers" situated in the Fighter Group Operations Rooms.

A movement section, comprised of Liaison Officers from Bomber and Coastal Commands, stationed in the Filter Room, was able to pass to the Controller details of time of departure and expected time of return of bomber and coastal formations. Thus, to some extent, it was possible to decide whether a track was hostile or friendly.

In addition, for the purpose of this exercise, returning aircraft were instructed to make an appropriate wireless signal when some 50 miles from the coast, a 'fix' being then obtained by directional wireless stations, and the information passed to the Liaison Officers.

A previously agreed symbol was then given to each track, the symbol determining the type of aircraft which the track was considered to be. Thus every recipient of the information of track and symbol received a simultaneous picture intelligible to each, both of the position of incoming raids and that of their suspected identity.

In this exercise, the first day's results were not so good as anticipated, but, as communications improved, so did the results, and, on the third day, the results were excellent. The symbols used on this occasion and, in fact, for some time after the outbreak of war, were as follows:

Aircraft known to be hostile – a numeral.
Bomber aircraft, friendly – double letters the first being R.
Fighter aircraft, friendly – letter F, followed by a numeral.
Doubtful aircraft, – letter X, followed by a numeral.

The task of the Observer Corps was firstly to pick up tracks told by the Radar system, as they made landfall, secondly to 'tell' upwards to Sectors and Groups the continued tracks of 'hostile' and of 'doubtful' aircraft (the Group Operations Room being responsible for onward telling to Fighter Command), and thirdly to pass forward from Observer Group to Observer Group tracks of friendly aircraft but not to tell the latter tracks upwards unless requested by a higher formation.

This latter task is obviously a matter of major difficulty when there are large number of aircraft flying. To assist in this, and for purposes of distinguishing the area of origin, each centre was given an initial letter corresponding as far as possible with the name of the Centre, e.g. C for Colchester etc. Any aircraft, or formation of aircraft, recognised as friendly was given a double letter symbol by the centre of the Observer Group in which the track originated, i.e. CA, CB etc. When it was not clear that the track could be identified as friendly and when it was not connected with a previous Radar track, the same letter of origin was used, followed by a numeral, e.g. C8, C9 etc., and this was changed to a double letter symbol when identified as friendly, the track being told upwards to Sectors and groups while still being unidentifiable and the telling being discontinued on a friendly identification being given.

Outbreak of War – Changed Conditions of Service

This exercise was invaluable, and the system used was still in force when, on August 24th, the Observer Corps was called out on duty, prior to the outbreak of war on September 3rd 1939. By this date the whole of the Northern, Midland, Southern and Western Areas had been completed, as also had the Scottish Area with the exception of Number 32 (Carlisle) and Number 38 (Aberdeen), while Number 37 Group (Dundee) was officially formed on October 18th.

Here it may be of interest to record that, on August 24th 1939, when the Corps was mobilised on a war time basis, changes in the status, conditions of service and remuneration came into operation, and these had been decided at an Inter-Departmental Committee consisting of representatives of the Air Ministry, Home Office, and Treasury, which had considered the subject following the crisis of 1938.

It was decided, at that conference, that the administration, recruitment and payment of volunteer members of the Observer Corps should pass from the Police to the Air Ministry and that the following changes should take place:

(a) They should relinquish their Special Constable status.
(b) They were to become entitled to a remuneration of 1/3d

an hour, with a maximum of £3 a week increased to £3.5.0 by award of 5/0d a week war bonus with effect from July 1st 1940.

(c) They were to be given an opportunity of applying for employment on a full-time basis of a 48 hour week, or of accepting part-time employment.

Chapter 5

The Outbreak of War to May 1941

At the outbreak of war it was naturally anticipated that there would be a considerable amount of activity, but for the first few months such activity as there was was confined almost entirely to the coastal groups on the East Coast of England and Scotland and, to a lesser extent, to those along the South Coast.

The first occasion on which the Observer Corps came into prominence was on October 16th 1939 when attacks were made on the Firth of Forth. Reconnaissance flights by the German Air Force began in the morning at 0927 hours. The main attacks, unheralded by R.D.F. warning, took place between 1400 and 1600 hours. There was a certain amount of duplication of Observer Corps plots, but it is believed that some 9 to 12 aircraft took part in this raid. The aircraft used were correctly identified by the Observer Corps as hostile. The attacks were made on the Forth Bridge and on naval vessels in the vicinity.

Again on the 20th of that month sound plots were recorded by the Observer Corps in the Forth area, believed to be enemy aircraft at a great height, though no aircraft were seen by the posts. An anti-aircraft gun position claimed, however, to have sighted a Heinkel 111 at 30,000 feet approximately.

During the ensuing weeks there were a few cases of identification of hostile aircraft by the coastal posts, for instance on October 30th, He.111 were identified which subsequently bombed a ship off the Goodwin Sands, and on the same day a Heinkel 111 was sighted near North Berwick.

On November 10th, posts in the Lancaster Observer Group identified a Heinkel as far inland as Hexham, and on December

6th the Horsham Group picked up a He.111, which had crossed in near Portsmouth, and subsequently was tracked East across England and flew out over the coast near Chelmsford.

Tracking and Plotting

In the main enemy aircraft which were seen overland at this early stage were single aircraft obviously on reconnaissance, and which naturally proved very difficult to intercept.

Apart from these reconnaissance aircraft the activity was confined to enemy aircraft which reconnoitred our East Coast convoys and provided the information for subsequent attacks. In consequence, the Observer Corps from Aberdeen down to the Channel were limited in their work mostly to fleeting glimpses of hostile aircraft some miles off the coast and to innumerable sound plots, which quite frequently turned out to be those of our own aircraft which were carrying out continual convoy patrols. There was a good deal of confusion in plotting due to the difficulty of distinguishing between these two types of aircraft.

This difficulty was very noticeable at this early period, but equally noticeable was the way in which Observer posts acquired later the facility for distinguishing not only between friendly and hostile aircraft, but even between different types of friendly and hostile. In this connection lies the importance of the "Cluster" system of posts, by which three posts (in most cases) share a common line to one plotter at the Observer centre. Thus each post hears what is said by its fellow posts and confirmation can be obtained of the opinion expressed by any one post.

In the light of the skill and accuracy acquired later by the Observer Corps the mistakes at this early stage show up more prominently, but it must be remembered that the knowledge and experience at this period had been acquired by infrequent practices, in many cases with civil aircraft hired for the occasion, and on only one full scale practice just prior to the outbreak of war. At this stage the tracking was in many cases very scrappy and disjointed, frequently duplicated (owing to faulty filtering and plotting at the Observer Centres) with surprising and mysterious "aircraft" tracks appearing when plotting was by sound. On one occasion a track given as "doubtful" was found to have followed exactly (and at a speed of 20 m.p.h.) the road from one village to another. On another occasion, a track plotted by sound as circling for a long time in a small area, was found to have been in a district where all-night ploughing was in progress. It is also a fact that the planet Venus was plotted visually, as an aircraft at 30,000 feet.

These, however, were early troubles and experience was gained rapidly, and there are very few of such mistakes recorded after the first year of war.

A major trouble which remained to some extent throughout the war, was the question of inter-centre handover of tracks. Great improvements were made with this question in 1942, at the time of the major re-organisation, but by that time the problem had also increased with the increase in the amount of friendly flying.

December 1939 – May 1940
From December 1939 up to May 1940, the activities of the Corps were confined, as has been said, almost entirely to reporting such enemy aircraft as could be seen or heard off the coast in connection with convoy reconnaissance or attacks on convoys, and also, at that time, to reporting gunfire heard, ships seen sinking or being bombed, and reconnaissance aircraft overland.

To show, however, that, even at this early stage, the Observer Corps was having some success with its sound tracking, the opinion may be quoted of the Senior Air Staff Officer, Fighter Command, who on January 21st 1940 wrote: "Please see Enclosure 2B, which is the track of a high flying Spitfire. This is the second occasion in a week that Observer Posts in East Anglia have picked up and plotted by sound a raid that crossed the coast at 30,000 feet. On this occasion the track was plotted further North than on January 18th so that a different set of posts sent in the reports. The track is not so good as that provided on January 18th, but is, however, very creditable, considering the great height and adverse weather".

The difficulties which had arisen in confusion between hostile tracks and those of our own aircraft going out to, or returning from patrols were, to a great extent, overcome by the issue of an instruction to R.A.F. Sectors to 'tell' to Observer Corps Centres, via the liaison lines, the movements of fighter aircraft which had been ordered to operate to seaward in the R.D.F. area, in addition to the movements of fighters inland. By this means, the Observer Corps Centres were enabled to filter the tracks produced by the posts, and a considerable improvement was noticeable in the nomenclature of raids.

During this period the only other instructions of importance issued to the Observer Corps were, firstly, that in the event of parachute raids on Great Britain, messages from the Observer Corps, on that subject, were to be passed to Sector Headquarters for onward transmission to Fighter Groups, and, secondly, that, in the event of an aircraft in distress being sighted, its position and course were to be reported to the Fighter Group, the information being passed thence to the Movement Liaison Section at Fighter Command. On the latter subject, it may be mentioned here that the services of the Observer Corps were of inestimable value (particularly in the later stages of the war) in providing the necessary information by which badly damaged bombers and fighters were enabled to make a safe landing.

Observer Corps Expansion: Formation of Nos. 20, 21, 28-1, 28-2, 33, 35, 39 Groups

With the fall of France it became apparent that enemy attacks might be expected in the West of England. It was also realised at that time that the Scottish coverage was inadequate. Accordingly schemes for expansion of the Observer Corps, which had been held in abeyance, were once again considered.

It was decided to form four Groups to cover Devon, Cornwall and Western Wales. These Groups were Number 20 (Yeovil), 21 (Exeter), 28-1 (Carmarthen) and 28-2 (Caernarvon). In Scotland three Groups were to be formed, namely Numbers 33 (Ayr), 35 (Oban) and 39 (Inverness).

To continue the story of the formation of these Groups and of their relation to the Fighter Groups of the Royal Air Force, on July 28th 1940 the position was summarised by Headquarters Fighter Command as follows:

Number 10 (Fighter) Group Area. Observer Group No. 21 (Exeter) now functioning. Observer Group No. 20 (Truro) being formed. The function of Number 20 Group mainly to identify and report aircraft movements off the Cornish coast direct to St. Eval.

Numbers 10 and 12 (Fighter) Group Areas:- Observer Group No. 28-1, to report aircraft movements in South Wales, on or off the coast, to Pembrey (subsequently changed to Carmarthen). No. 28-2, to report aircraft movements in North Wales to the Wrexham Centre (subsequently changed to Caernarvon). Both these Groups were eventually to change into normal Groups with ordinary tracking.

Number 13 (Fighter) Group Area:- When communications become available, a similar coastal reporting Group will be formed to cover the North and East Coasts of Scotland, roughly north of Dernoch.

Observer Groups Numbers 39 (Inverness), 35 (Oban), and 33 (Ayr) being formed.

For most of the Groups it will be seen that the procedure adopted was to start with an identification and reporting system reporting either to Royal Air Force Stations or to Observer Corps Centres, and subsequently to develop this into a full Observer Group with a normal tracking and plotting system.

The above mentioned Groups were all completed at varying dates during the year 1940.

The Battle of Britain
Until May 1940 it had been assumed that single-engine aircraft could be regarded as friendly if seen over the English coast, but with the rapid advance of the enemy through France and the Low Countries this could no longer apply. On May 15th 1940, the following information was passed to the Observer Corps:-

"As England is now within range of hostile single-engine aircraft, single-engine aircraft from now on are not necessarily to be regarded as friendly".

The months of comparative inactivity for the posts and centres of the Observer Corps were drawing to an end, and, on May 18th 1940, Headquarters Fighter Command issued this signal to all Groups within the Command: "German High Command threaten reprisals for our bombing in Germany last night, in which they say we attacked open towns. This is significant, and heavy attacks on this country must be expected in the immediate future".

This forecast of impending heavy air attacks on these islands began to be fulfilled in July 1940, and from then on the real testing of the Observer Corps began. It was fortunate from their point of view that they had had nine months in which to find their feet at a war time status. Apart from the occasional hostile tracks which they had told and plotted up to that date, they had also had daily practices in which all aircraft appearing (friendly or otherwise) were told from posts to centres, and from centres to sectors, groups, and finally to Fighter Command. Thus they acquired skill and accuracy during the nine months of comparative inaction.

During July and the beginning of August 1940, the German attacks swung more to the South and East, and were directed against targets such as ports and coastal shipping in these areas, though raids were not lacking against inland targets, mostly by single aircraft or by small formations of enemy aircraft. These were by day, while by night the targets were widely dispersed, chiefly in the West, in Wales, and on coastal districts in the East by small formations of bombers; while minelaying, of course, continued regularly throughout the whole period.

It was the night period that naturally was of the most value at this time from the standpoint of the Observer as, in the usual weather condition in this country, it frequently happens that tracking can only be by sound. It was not the practice at that time to do other than give a track when working by sound alone, while estimates of height, strength, and direction were omitted. Naturally the last three items were of value to the R.A.F., and Sectors were continually asking that this information should be supplied, though the Observer Corps were at first reluctant to supply this information, owing to the possibility of considerable error, pressure was exerted by the Research Group, known as the Operational Research Section (which had come to Fighter Command from Bawdsey at the beginning of the war, and which was already in close touch with the Observer Corps).

The O.R.S. recommended strongly that the R.A.F. controller would be (in this instance) better off with approximate information than with no information on these three points at all. They considered also that, from their experience of Observers, the average observer was able, with experience, to estimate strength and height with an accuracy and reliability worth having.

Accordingly it was decided that heights were to be told to the nearest 5000 feet at first (i.e. 1000, 5000, 10000 etc.), and that directions of tracks were also to be told, though no strength was as yet to be given. (This last item of information was supplied at a later date).

At the end of the war an estimate of the quality and capacity of the Observer Corps under non-busy conditions was as follows:

Height   Visual, average error 10% (less reliable above 20,000 ft.); by sound, average error 20% (reliability varies markedly between Groups).

Number of aircraft Visual, exact by sound, good estimate.

Both day and night attacks increased in scale during the second and third weeks of August 1940, though again they were directed at the same types of targets, and by now most of the Observer Groups, particularly in the manufacturing areas and round the great ports, had had a considerable amount of experience in tracking, and in distinguishing friend from foe; Leeds, Bristol, Birmingham, Portland, Portsmouth and many other places had been visited either by day of by night.

Then, during the next two weeks, the third phase of the Battle of Britain, the German plan started to develop, and by day the Southern Area, by night the Northern and Midland Areas of the Observer Corps came into action in the intensive attacks that now took place. These were directed by day against Number 11 (Fighter) group's airfields, and by night against Merseyside and the Midlands. In those two weeks by day the German Air Force sorties totalled in the neighbourhood of 8000, and by night there were usually some 200 enemy aircraft over this country.

It is difficult during the accounts of these air battles both by day and by night to single out any one action of the Observer Corps for comment, as the essential feature of their work was the necessity for steady, accurate plotting and estimation of the heights and strength of enemy formations. Quick and accurate recognition of whether the aircraft were hostile or friendly was of paramount importance as was the ability to identify the varying types. It may be truly said, though, that in cases where successful interceptions were made, and where aircraft were shot down by our fighters overland, a very high proportion of the credit was due to the Observer Corps, linked up as it was with the whole system of defence, and providing at that time the only means of tracking down and intercepting aircraft by day, and the principal means by night. It must be remembered, too, that once enemy aircraft had passed inland from the R.D.F. area, the plots and tracks provided by the Observer Corps furnished the information on which decisions were made as to the issue of Air Raid Warnings, which were, at that time, issued centrally from Headquarters, Fighter Command.

Covering, as the Observer Corps did, almost the whole land area of the country (except, in fact, for the North West of Scotland) with posts spaced from 6 to 10 miles apart, they were able to render quick reports of bombs dropped, aircraft shot down, parachutes descending, flares seen, and so on, while the coastal posts were frequently in a position not only to report attacks on shipping, but, in the case of aircraft being shot down, to furnish most valuable information, at the time of the occurrence, which led in many cases to the saving of pilots' lives.

On September 6th the night activity was concentrated on London and Merseyside, and from then onwards, through September and October, London was the main objective of the German night attacks, though other parts of the country, notably Merseyside, Lancashire and South Wales had their visitations also. By day the enemy offensive lessened in scale, though attacks continued to be made on London, September 15th being the day of the heaviest attack.

From September 17th the fighter and fighter-bomber sweeps began, coming in over Kent and proceeding towards London. These sweeps continued by day during September and October. Also towards the end of September heavy daylight bombing attacks were made against aircraft factories in the South and South-west of England, in the areas of Southampton and the Solent, Plymouth and Bristol.

During the period of the Battle of Britain it will be of interest to record a typical period of activity for the plotting and tracking of which the Observer Corps was responsible, such as that on August 18th when, though the tracks recorded show a total of 2600 enemy sorties, it is probable that a reasonable total was about 2000.

On that day the following programme of the day's offensive gives a good idea of the number of Observer Groups which were involved, apart altogether from the subsequent night activity which covered the areas round Rugby, Birmingham, Liverpool, Lincolnshire and South Wales:

11.00 hrs.
Dover and East Kent.   Observer Groups 1, 2, 19

11.00-13.00 hrs.
Activity off Lands' End.   Observer Group 20

13.00 hrs.
Newcastle and Sunderland.   Observer Groups 9, 30

13.30 hrs.
Scarborough and Hull.   Observer Groups 9, 10

15.00 Hrs.
Essex.   Observer Groups 18, 19

15.30 hrs.
Dover.   Observer Group 1

17.00 hrs.
Isle of Wight and Inland.   Observer Groups 2, 3

18.00 hrs.
Dover and Inland   Observer Groups 1, 2, 3, 19
(across to Croydon and Farnborough).

Plotting Difficulties and their Solution
One quotation taken from the Form 'Y' dated August 20th 1940 is

of interest in that it points to one of the main difficulties experienced by all concerned in Operations Room work. It runs as follows: "There were an unusual number of raids picked up inland by the Observer Corps with no previous tracking".

All raids tracked by R.D.F. bore a distinctive lettering and numbering indicating their believed identification, e.g. hostile, friendly, doubtful and so on. The Observer Corps then carried on these tracks when they crossed inland with the designation affixed by R.D.F. unless a visual identification caused them to alter such designation. Any tracks missed by R.D.F. which appeared overland without previous tracking, were until identified, given a letter (corresponding to the Observer Centre) and a number (of which 1 to 9 were allotted to each centre). If the track was later recognised as hostile the Observer Centre changed this letter and number to one of a block of numbers which had been allocated to each fighter group. This change was made on instructions received from the Observer Corps Liaison Officer in the Fighter Group Operations Room. If, on the other hand, the track was subsequently recognised as friendly, the telling of it onwards was discontinued.

The Air Officer Commanding-in-Chief, in a letter to all Fighter Groups, drew attention to the persistence of tracks originated by the Observer Corps and bearing their special lettering. As he said, it was impossible for an enemy raid to originate in this country and therefore, when one of those Observer Corps plots appeared on the table, it must be either

(a) a raid which had been previously plotted and then lost, or
(b) a raid which had not been previously picked up by the R.D.F. or by the Observer Corps, or
(c) a friendly aircraft

In his opinion there was a tendency for the Observer Corps to cover themselves by reporting tracks which they had no real reason to suppose to be hostile, and also a very definite shirking of their responsibility by Group Controllers who allowed that state of indecision to persist indefinitely.

No Observer Corps Controller should allow a new plot to be told to a Group or Sector Operations table unless he had some good reason for supposing it to be hostile. He should normally offer his explanation (to the O.C.L.O.) at the same time at which he authorised the telling of the track.

It was then the responsibility of the Group Controller, working through his staff, to make an early decision as to whether to permit the continued telling of the track or not, and, if the former, to decide under what designation it should continue to be told. It was the responsibility of the Lost Raid Officer (at a later stage known as the Raids Intelligence Officer and finally as the Raids Recognition Officer) to decide whether it was possible to 'marry' it up with a track which had previously been lost, and to advise the Group Controller accordingly.

It will be obvious that, despite the coverage of the Observer Corps, it would be quite possible, owing to configuration of the land or owing to adverse weather conditions, for tracks to be lost for some miles and for small formations to break away from main raids, in either case to appear later as new tracks, and, despite all efforts, this continued to be a difficulty which was never entirely overcome.

Arising out of this point is another of the factors which complicated the picture as it appeared on Operations Rooms Tables. A large formation of hostile aircraft would frequently split into a number of smaller formations, either owing to a pre-arranged plan or by reason of interceptions carried out by our fighter aircraft. In order to maintain the identity of the original raid it was laid down that "if an enemy raid splits, the main portion retains the raid number and the several formations which split off are denoted by a suffix letter added to the original raid number. These letters are allotted by the Observer Centre".

It will be realised that, on the occasions of mass attacks on this country, such as those during the Battle of Britain, the picture presented was liable to be somewhat confused, more especially as on many occasions the bulk of the hostile aircraft was being tracked over a small area such as Kent.

It was as a result of a number of cases in which important information regarding enemy tracks, either failed entirely to appear on Group or Command Operations Tables, or only in part and after undue delay, that the Commander-in-Chief took steps to see what measures could be taken to reduce such failures.

Realising that these failures were due to the plotting approaching saturation point owing to enemy mass attacks, the conclusion reached was that telling must be selective, and that the teller must understand the point of view of the Operations Room to which he 'told'.

He therefore appointed a Royal Air Force officer to act as observer in the Operations Room of Number 11 (F) Group, and two members of the Scientific Research Section (later the Operational Research Section) to work with the Observer Corps Centres. It was to be remembered that it was an equal intention to procure the correct information as speedily as possible for use in connection with the operation of fighters, as it was to procure information for Command for the purpose of issuing air raid warnings. It is only necessary to say here that the close association between the Operational Research Section and the Observer Corps continued from this time onwards throughout the war, and proved invaluable in speeding up and in simplifying the procedure both in speech-telling and in teleprinting, and, by their recommendations, in altering the system of telling so that the maximum possible use was made of the information supplied by the Observer Corps.

The Raids Intelligence Officer and the Observer Corps Liaison Officer

Mention has been made both of the Raids Intelligence Officer (later known as the Raids Recognition Officer) and of the Observer Corps Liaison Officer and, as the work of both was intimately concerned with correct track production and designation of raids, it is necessary to describe in detail their duties before proceeding to a study of the Night Raids. Minor amendments were made in their functions and in the procedure which they employed, but, in essence, the duties as laid down on October 16th 1940 were virtually unchanged in so far as they apply to the points specified in this section of Battle Orders.

The Duties of the Raids Intelligence Officer (R.I.O.) and the Observer Corps Liaison Officer (O.C.L.O.) were of such a nature that, though they were separately defined in Battle Orders, they were most intimately connected in actual operations. While the R.I.O.(later known as the Raids Recognition Officer, or R.R.O.) being a member of the Royal Air Force, was officially responsible for the Fighter Group Operations Table procedure and for the direction of those working on the floor of the Operations Room (the plotters, tellers and so on), and the O.C.L.O. was responsible to the Fighter Group Controller for the working of the Observer Corps system and procedure, it was obviously necessary that each should understand thoroughly the other's work, and should, when necessary, be able to deputise unofficially when his colleague was already fully employed. Such, in fact, was the method adopted, and the arrangement was, in actual practice, remarkably satisfactory. There were, in other words, jointly responsible for producing, for the benefit of the Fighter Controller and his staff, a picture on the Operations Room Table on which the Controller could base his decisions for the disposition of the aircraft under his command.

Change of Tactics of the German Air Force
With the introduction of fighter and fighter-bomber sweeps towards London a new phase of the Battle of Britain may be said to have started, while the heavy night attacks on London continued, developing later into concentrated attacks on other towns of major importance in industry and in the production of armaments and equipment. Another feature of this period, during October, was the use of single bombers to attack important targets in London and the Midlands.

Change in Telling Procedure
It proved necessary at this period to introduce a new system of telling procedure for the Observer Corps, a system that was tried out first in the Number 11 (Fighter) Group Area (the area of maximum activity) and was later, on December 8th, 1940, standardized in all Groups throughout the Command. This method of telling was adopted to differentiate between the tracks of hostile bombers and fighters whenever the Observer Corps were able to distinguish between them. When the observer post could differentiate, the Observer Corps Centre told the raid

information by teleprinter in the normal manner adding the letters ZF (enemy fighters) or ZB (enemy bombers) after the height. In the case of speech telling the words "enemy fighters" or "enemy bombers" were used. When the raid consisted of bombers escorted by fighters the bomber identification ZB was given. If the fighter escort broke away, or was drawn off by our fighters, the raid was told as a "split raid". Using the identification "ZF" or "ZB" as appropriate.

This system proved of great value to Controllers both at Sector and at Groups, for the interception of hostile raids, more especially where large forces of bombers and fighters were employed by the enemy. It enabled the Group controller to allocate his forces to the best advantage, while Sectors had prior information of the type of raid with which they would be confronted.

The Heavy Night Attacks

The story of the heavy night attacks on this country has been told elsewhere, and, in this narrative, it is only necessary to mention particular details when they resulted in a change in the procedure of the Observer Corps. It will be not out of place, however, to place on record the fact that, for the men at the Observer Posts and Centres, the strain to which they were subjected was considerable. The men at the posts were on many occasions seeing bombs fall, and telling aircraft plotted in the very places where they knew their homes to be, while they had to remain at their posts and centres until their tours of duty were completed. That this fact was appreciated by those in authority is exemplified by the messages sent on several occasions by the Air Officer Commanding-in-Chief during the periods of enemy night bombing activity.

The following message sent by A.O.C.-in-C. to the Commandant of the Observer Corps is typical: "I have heard with great satisfaction of the excellent work carried out by the personnel of Number 23 Observer Group Centre (Bristol) on the night of the 24th/25th November. Please convey my congratulations to the Controllers and crews of the Centre on their performance and spirit of determination. That members reported at the Centre in spite of extreme difficulties and in several cases when they had sustained material loss is particularly noteworthy".

This was on the occasion of the heavy attack on Bristol and Clifton when enemy aircraft from the Cherbourg area made land-fall between Portland and the Isle of Wight and dropped at least 2000 incendiary bombs together with a number of High Explosive. Considerable damage was done to communications, industrial plant and public utilities. This was, of course, only one of many, and certainly by no means the heaviest of raids, but the occasion is typical of the many occasions on which personnel had to leave their house during a raid, in some cases when their homes had been already damaged, and had to take up their work knowing, with considerable accuracy, that their relatives were still in danger.

During October 1940, London was not free of bombing for a single night and in the latter half of the month many of the big cities were attacked. Coventry and Birmingham were bombed heavily during the last fortnight of the month, while Liverpool, Manchester, Hull and Glasgow also had their share, though not on such a heavy scale.

Forthcoming Changes in the Reporting Method
It was during this period that the limitations both of the R.D.F system and of the Observer Corps system became obvious in relation to their capacity for dealing with very large numbers of enemy aircraft individually, and it was as a direct result of this discovery that the Macroscopic Reporting Method was brought into force in the summer of 1941. This method dealt with the R.D.F. system of reporting three types of hostile activity:

(i) *Crocodile raids* – in which aircraft in close succession follow tracks lying within a narrow channel.
(ii) *Mass Raids* – in which a large number of aircraft are in formation.
(iii) *Random activity* – in which a large number of aircraft are flying at random. This case includes all types not covered in (i) and (ii) above.

These types of activity, where it became impossible to report tracks individually by the usual method, were to be reported as 'Area raids' showing the following details:

(i)   The approximate area covered.
(ii) An estimate of the total number of aircraft.
(iii) Under certain conditions the general direction of flight.
(iv) Under certain conditions the mean height or the upper and lower limits of height.

In order to tell such an area, and to ensure that it was plotted in Group and Sector Operations Rooms, the four corners of a quadrilateral were told, movement of the area of activity being indicated as required by telling changes of the positions of one or more corners.

As the enemy aircraft started to make landfall, and thus to pass from R.D.F area into that covered by the Observer Corps, it became the duty of the latter to deal with the situation. In certain cases the "Area Raids" could become "Battle Zones" where it proved impossible to distinguish individual tracks. If it was still possible to do so, Observer Centres had to tell individual formations when they reached the Coast and emerged from the R.D.F. "Area". In that case they would allot each track a Centre designation according to the identification given to the raid.

The Fighter-Bomber Raids

The tactics employed by the German Air Force in October 1940 proved most difficult to counter. By day S.E. England was very rarely free of enemy aircraft. The enemy fighters were usually at a height of over 20,000 feet before reaching the coast of Kent. At this height the R.D.F. cover was not infallible and it was possible for the enemy to reach the Kentish coast before our aircraft could attain the necessary height for interception. Once over the coast, the cloudy weather in October and the height of the hostile aircraft made the tracking of the Observer Corps liable to considerable error, and rendered extremely difficult the task of distinguishing between the fighter and the fighter-bomber formations.

From the point of view of the Royal Air Force, shadowing

aircraft were used, from October 9th, whose task it was to reconnoitre and shadow enemy formations, reporting the information obtained, by V.H.F. R/T. By this method a good deal of very valuable information was obtained. Standing patrols were also used on fixed patrol lines, and by this means, though a wasteful one, it proved possible to gain the necessary height to deal with enemy attacks.

The most intensive period of this form of activity passed in the second week of November, and the German Air Force then returned to their attacks on Coastal towns and shipping.

Passing of the Night Attacks on London

As has been said, the night attacks on London continued throughout the whole of October and, in fact, with great regularity during the first three weeks of November, but with the heavy attack on Coventry on the night of 14th/15th November, the tactics had changed again. Though enemy aircraft still visited London by night, the majority passed overhead on their way to the great Midland towns.

Every part of the Observer system was put to its greatest test during the ensuing three months. Between the end of October 1940 and February 1941 many large towns received intensive raids, and almost nightly streams of enemy aircraft crossed in either from Cherbourg north over Western England, or over Kent and Sussex travelling northwest, or in over the east or north-east coast. Despite the many difficulties of track production and continuation, of recognition and identification, and of working (never underground) in conditions of considerable danger, the Observer Corps certainly 'earned its keep' as one of the most important factors in the Air Defence System of Great Britain.

Formation of the North-Western Area

With the organisation of new Observer Groups to cover Devon, Cornwall and Western Wales the administrative work was becoming too great to be dealt with by the Western Area Headquarters as then constituted, dealing as they were with ten Observer Groups. The decision was therefore made to form a new area in the North-West, so this would also fit in better with the expansion of the Royal Air Force, who were forming a new

Fighter Group (number 9), in the North-West of England. It was decided to separate Numbers 28-2, 26 and 27 Groups from the Western Area, and, together with Number 7 Group (from the Northern area), place them under a new Area Headquarters conveniently situated, the area of these four groups to coincide more or less with that of Number 9 (F) Group of the Royal Air Force. This new formation left six Observer Groups in the Western Area, covering the area of Number 10 (F) Group of the Royal Air Force.

Transfer of Number 33 group to Northern Area
On April 17th 1941 it was decided that Number 33 Group (Ayr) should be transferred from the Scottish to the Northern Area, and that this was to take effect from April 20th.

Organisation on June 3rd 1941
These various changes were completed and the following table shows the state of Groups and Areas by June 1941:

Headquarters	Bentley Priory, Stanmore
Commandant	Air Commodore A.D. Warrington-Morris C.M.G., O.B.E. (retd.)
Western Area Headquarters:	Gloucester
Area Commandant:	Air Commodore E.A.D. Masterman CB, CMG, OBE, AFC, (retd.)
Group Numbers:	20, 21, 22, 23, 24, 25, 28-1
Southern Area Headquarters:	Uxbridge
Area Commandant:	Group Captain I.T. Courtney, C.B.E. (retd.)
Group Numbers:	1, 2, 3, 4, 17, 18, 19
Midland Area Headquarters:	Grantham
Area Commandant:	Group Captain V.O. Rees, O.B.E. (retd.)
Group Numbers:	5, 6, 11, 12, 14, 15, 16.

Northern Area Headquarters:Catterick
Area Commandant: Air Commodore A.L. Godman,
          C.M.G., D.S.O. (retd.)
Group Numbers: 8, 9, 10, 29, 30, 32, 33

Scottish Area Headquarters: Edinburgh
Area Commandant: Air Commodore R.P. Ross D.S.O.,
          A.F.C. (retd.)
Group Numbers: 31, 34, 35, 36, 37, 38, 39.

North Western Area HQ: Barton, Nr. Preston.
Area Commandant: Colonel V.O. Robinson, O.B.E.,
          M.C. (retd.)
Group Numbers: 7, 26, 27, 28-2

The only additional Group formed was Number 40 Group with its centre at Portree in the Isle of Skye.

Chapter 6

May 1941 to December 1941

It is of interest to note that from May onwards the strategic interests of the enemy had shifted from the Western Area, the bulk of his striking force had been removed and he concentrated for the remainder of the year on the blockade of Great Britain. Instead of attacking ports and towns with large forces he used small forces in shipping attacks and minelaying. In attacking inland towns he avoided heavily defended areas in his approach. This was by night, while the day fighter sweeps continued over the area of Kent during the month of June, but after the first week in July, as our own fighter offensive increased, the enemy fighters stayed on their own side of the channel.

Night Activity
The scale of night attacks dropped progressively from 200 to 300 sorties per night in the first half of May to 30 sorties per night in August, and 22 sorties per night in December 1941. In the first half of May attacks took place on ports and industrial areas in the Mersey, Clyde, Belfast and Midlands districts, culminating in widespread bombing by 250 aircraft on the night of 11th/12th May, which really finished the big night bombing offensive that had begun in September 1940.

Ports and towns on the East, West and South coasts still received attacks from time to time by small enemy forces, but a great part of the night effort was directed against shipping. Hull was a favourite target during this period, but the provision of a dazzle barrage formed of a concentration of searchlights, in August, caused considerable inaccuracy in bomb aiming. The enemy took advantage of the moon periods during the latter half of the year, but our night defensive effort was becoming considerably more effective, and these attacks became progressively more expensive. Intruder activity continued during the summer and early autumn, but ceased in late autumn with the transfer of the Intruder unit to the Mediterranean theatre of operations.

The Day Offensive
The Royal Observer Corps had very little reporting of enemy activity to do during the daylight hours for the last 8 months of 1941, as the scale of the enemy effort declined from an average of 74 sorties a day in the month of May to 21 sorties a day in July. During the last half of the year the average number of enemy sorties daily was 10 to 12 reconnaissance flights, one or two being over land and the remainder on shipping, while there were very occasional long-range bomber attacks on shipping, or on land targets. The policy adopted by the enemy, by day as by night, was blockade.

Running Commentaries.
One of the methods by which more use was made of the Observer Corps information during this period was the employment of running commentaries in interceptions. The existing method of effecting interceptions was by the vectoring of fighters, whose positions were plotted by "fixes" obtained by Sectors, while those of the enemy aircraft were plotted on Observer Corps information. By the use of these two systems there were naturally differences in time-lag, apart altogether from possible errors, due to the human element, in fixer stations and in Observer Corps Centres. Also the problem of the difficulty experienced by the Observer Corps posts in giving exact heights at high altitudes was always present.

It was therefore decided to attempt to use one source of information only, when conditions of visibility were favourable, and thus eliminate differences in time lag, while positional errors, with reference to the ground, would be purely relative.

At Observer Centres, where liaison lines existed to Sectors, the Duty Controller, on seeing from the plotting that fighters had approached to within 10 miles of the enemy raid, and considering that a running commentary was practicable, would say to the Sector Controller or Operations Officer, "Urgent Running Commentary".

The Table Supervisor (in the Observer Corps Centre) would then plug into the plotter's position, connected to the Posts reporting the hostile aircraft, and would, from what he heard from the Posts, give all the assistance possible to the Duty Controller, who would pass information directly to the Sector Controller for use in controlling his fighters. The information was to be given on the following points:

(a)   The relative positions, courses and heights of the friendly fighters and the enemy, and the distance between them.

(b)   Any alteration in the course and height of the hostile aircraft.

(c)   Information concerning the weather in the area, including cloud conditions, and whether the hostile aircraft appeared to be making for or entering cloud banks.

(d)   The relative position of the hostile aircraft to any A.A. shell bursts observed.

If a running commentary had been commenced and the action appeared likely to pass into an adjacent Observer Group area, the adjacent centre was to be given adequate notice of the fact that the running commentary system was in use.

This system would be impracticable during intensive enemy action but was admirably suited, in conditions of favourable visibility, for the interception of single raiders or of small enemy formations, in fact the type of enemy action that was in force during a large part of 1941.

At the time of the introduction of running commentaries it was realised, too, that Observer Corps Centres and Ports were obtaining insufficient opportunity of plotting high flying aircraft, and Sector Controller were instructed to co-operate with Observer Corps Centre Controllers in providing for the information of posts, the height of fighter aircraft flying at 6,000 feet or more. By this means the posts were enabled to correct the heights which they had estimated, and acquire the facility of judging heights more accurately.

The system of running commentaries was, on the whole, very successful, though naturally its principal value was during the daylight hours. That it was possible also to achieve success by night is exemplified by a successful action that took place, on the night of April 8th/9th 1941, in the area of the Aberdeen Observer Centre. The report of the controller may be quoted verbatim – "Last night we had a great success with the running commentary, and the fighter made contact in poorish moonlight and some cloud when the visibility was not more than a mile and a half and then only for silhouettes. The bandit (i.e. enemy aircraft) was not definitely seen to fall into the sea but, as the pilot was exhausting his ammunition, a large portion of the plane flew off, past the fighter's wind-shield and the bandit took a lurch seawards. It was impossible to keep an accurate note of the messages sent by running commentary but two of them were as follows:

"Bandit on same track one mile east"
"Both planes same height same direction. Bandit just behind."

This was the last message given as the fighter swung round in a short circle and immediately made contact…..This has given great satisfaction throughout the whole centre in view of the misfortune we have been having recently with the low-flying Junkers which come in looking for ships."

Flight of Rudolf Hess

On Saturday, May 10th 1941, at about 22.10 hours a raid was being tracked in by R.D.F. towards the Northumbrian coast at 12,000 feet. This aircraft was first heard by a coastal post in No. 30 Observer Group (Durham Centre) at 22.23 hours. This track was continued across No. 30 Observer Group's Operations Table. On its inward journey the aircraft must have lost height rapidly for, at about 22.30 hours, it was seen by the crew of the post at Chatton who reported it as a Me.110, flying at 50 feet. This identification was naturally (considering the range of a Me.110) regarded by the Controller of the Centre and by No. 13 (F) Group Headquarters as highly improbable. At 22.32 hours the aircraft passed into No. 31 Observer Group (Galashiels centre) where it was continuously tracked until reaching the unobserved area in the Forest of Ettrick at 22.36 hours.

At about 22.35 hours two posts at Jedburgh and Ashkirk had caught a glimpse of the aircraft which was then reported as being a Me.110 at 5,000 feet.

Plotting by sound recommended at 22.45 hours in No. 34 Observer Group (Glasgow Centre), and here there was some confusion with a Defiant which was flying in the same area and consequently the track was given the Centre designation letter and number reserved for unidentified tracks.

The track was continued westward until the aircraft was again seen by a post at West Kilbride, where it was again recognised as hostile. Here the post were unable to give a definite identification, but considered that it might be a Do.215. The aircraft, after flying low over the coast, turned back towards Glasgow at a height of between 4,000 and 5,000 feet. It was then reported by the post at Eaglesham to have crashed in flames near Bonnyton Moor, a few miles south-west of Glasgow at 23.09 hours.

The Assistant Group Officer of No. 34 Group who was in the Glasgow Centre at the time, and who suspected that the aircraft was a Me.110 owing to its high speed, then motored to the scene of the crash, examined the wreckage and confirmed his suspicions. He interviewed the pilot and recognised him as Rudolf Hess, though the prisoner gave the false name of Hauptmann Alfred Horn.

The remainder of the story is well known, but this account of the flight deserves place in a narrative of the Observer Corps, illustrating as it does excellent plotting and tracking by posts, and accuracy in identification of an aircraft of a type which was completely unexpected over Scotland.

Appreciation of this, both to the Observer Posts and to the A.G.O. was conveyed in a letter from the Director of Fighter Operations on June 4th 1941, in which he said "The accuracy with which the aircraft was identified is commendable having regard to the fact that the appearance of an Me.110 in these areas was most unusual".

Change in Status of the Observer Corps
At this point it may be as well to record the following statement, made by the Secretary of State for Air, in the House of Commons

in April, 1941: "I am happy to inform the House that in recognition of the valuable services rendered by the Observer Corps over a number of years, His Majesty the King has been graciously pleased to approve that the Corps shall henceforth be known by the style and description of 'The Royal Observer Corps' ".

Interception in the Sub-Stratsphere

During the latter half of 1941 the problem of interception of enemy aircraft at sub-stratosphere heights was under discussion at Headquarters, Fighter Command, and plans were prepared for dealing with that form of attack. It was considered that an aircraft operating at such a height might not be observed by the Royal Observer Corps, and it was decided that reliance would have to be placed on G.C.I. (Ground Controlled Interception) Stations for the plotting and tracking both of the enemy aircraft and of the intercepting fighters. It is unnecessary in this narrative to give details of the Fighter Command scheme except in so far as it affected the Royal Observer Corps. In the case of the Centres, plots both of the enemy aircraft and of the intercepting fighters were to be received via their Sector Liaison lines. This information was then to be plotted on the Centre tables and broadcast through the normal channels to Sectors, Groups and Fighter Command. Suitable arrangements were made at Centres to enable the information received to be plotted on the main plotting table.

Central control was to be effected at Fighter Command from the information shown on the Fighter Command Operations Table, which would include G.C.I. and information received from Royal Observer Corps Centre. This Central Control would allocate the task of interception between Area Controls, which were to be set up at Number 9 and 11 Fighter Groups and at Colerne and Digby. Area Control Plotting Tables were to be established at these four areas, which would be connected direct to the appropriate G.C.I. Station. The information passed to the Royal Observer Corps Centres was to be obtained by Sectors monitoring the G.C.I. – Area Control Lines, and relaying such information to Centres via the Sector Centre liaison lines as stated above.

It was intended that exercises should be carried out under this plan, and this was in fact done on may subsequent occasions, though the original premise that sub-stratosphere flights would not be detected by the Royal Observer Corps did not appear to be well founded. Granted good conditions of visibility and an absence of low-flying aircraft (the sound of whose engines would blanket the sound of the sub-stratosphere aircraft) it proved possible both to see and hear the high flying aircraft.

An instruction was therefore issued by the Commandant that Centres were to plot on their tables information receive by sight and sound from Observer Posts. A filtered track was then to be broadcast in the normal manner by the Fighter Group Teller, Sector Teller and Teleprinter Operator. If the two types of plots did not coincide (of the sub-stratosphere aircraft), the Tellers should "Tell" the grid square of the leading counter. If there was a lateral difference in position the grid square of the G.C.I. plot should be given preference unless visual plots were being given by post crews.

As there might be some doubt, in the early stages, as to which fighter was carrying out the interception, tracks of fighters were not to be told unless called for by the Fighter Group.

For the purposes of practice interceptions, known by the code name of "Practice Quarry", it was decided to use a Fortress aircraft to represent the enemy bomber. This Fortress was to be based at Colerne and the intention of the trials was to ascertain what R.D.F. coverage existed at sub-stratosphere heights and to exercise the plotting and control organisation. Therefore, subject to the avoidance of enemy territory, approach to the areas would be made from as far as possible to seaward, and the Fortress was to fly as high as possible above 30,000 feet. It was considered that the enemy were developing aircraft which could fly up to, and possibly above 40,000 feet, and we were developing fighters with a performance which enabled such aircraft to be intercepted.

It will be of interest to record one such exercise, which took place on March 25th 1942. The Fortress took off from Colerne and was well plotted by the Observer Corps throughout. Bristol and, later, Cardiff picked up the aircraft and soon established a track. In the Truro and Exeter areas R.O.C. plots were well ahead of those given by G.C.I. and a good track was maintained by Yeovil and Bristol. Intercepting fighters were picked up by Truro long before G.C.I. and were well plotted by Exeter, Yeovil and Bristol. This, however, was only the second of the Quarry exercises, and as time went on not only did the G.C.I. improve, but it was found that the communications system, which involved using the Sector-Centre Liaison lines for the passing of G.C.I. plots to Observer Centres, was not entirely satisfactory, as the lines could not under those circumstances be used for any other purpose. During busy periods this was unsatisfactory.

It was accordingly decided that the G.C.I. plots should be used only, and R.O.C. plots would only be used if the scheme were to break down. This decision was first taken in Number 10 Fighter Group in May 1942, but by February 1943 it was universally applied and the Commandant stated 'It is realised by all concerned that the plotting of very high flying aircraft is outside the normal function of the R.O.C. A very complete arrangement exists for the interception of high flying raids by G.C.I. Stations, but this procedure is outside the scope of the R.O.C.'

"Bullseye" and "Dark" Raids

During the year 1941, with the improvement in our night defensive technique, it became necessary to devise methods to eliminate the risk of confusion between fighters in the interception of enemy aircraft. It was important that, where a fighter was engaged in intercepting a raid, that fact should be known to all concerned in order to preclude a second engagement of the raid, with consequent danger to the original fighter.

It was, therefore, decided that the Royal Observer Corps and the R.D.F. Filter Rooms should tell fighter-engaged raids under a special designation, and that such raids would be indicated in Group and Sector Operations Rooms by a special plaque. A raid engaged by a fighter with the co-operation of searchlights was to be told as a "Bullseye" raid; a raid engaged by a G.C.I. controlled fighter, on which searchlights were not to expose, was to be known as a "Dark" raid.

In the case of a "Bullseye" raid responsibility of informing the appropriate Observer Centre that a particular raid had been allotted the symbol "Bullseye" was the responsibility of the Sector Controller, the authority whose duty it was to decide that the raid was to be engaged.

In the case of a "Dark" raid, it was the duty of the G.C.I. controller deciding to engage a raid to pass the information to the Sector Controller, who having verified that the raid in question was not already "Bullseye" or "Dark" was responsible for informing the Observer Centre that the raid was "Dark". Arrangements were, of course, made for the procedure required to terminate a "Bullseye" or a "Dark" raid, in cases where a fighter destroyed, lost, or broke away from a raid, the appropriate Observer Centre being informed of the fact.

Raid Strength in Tracking by Sound
It has been mentioned previously that, on October 17th 1940, at the suggestion of the Operational Research Section, height and direction was to be told by the Royal Observer Corps when plotting was by sound. Operations Procedure Order No. 35 laid down that, from November 1941, the Royal Observer Corps when telling "heard" plots, were, where possible, to give an estimate of the number of aircraft forming the raid. It was emphasised that the figure given would be an estimate only, based by the Observer Centre on the personal judgement and experience of the observers hearing the raid, and would thus be analogous to "counting" by the R.D.F. The number scale was to be used (e.g. 1, 1+, 2, 3, 3+ etc.), and in the case of "F", "Dark" or "Bullseye" raids the strength of the raid would be the estimate total number of aircraft present, including friendly fighters.

The Employment of Long Aerial Mines – "Mutton" Operation
Another operation in which the services of the Royal Observer Corps were utilized during the year under consideration was known by the code name of "Mutton". This operation entailed the laying of aerial mine curtains, either over land or sea in the path of approaching hostile raiders. The mine curtain would be lethal for 15 to 20 minutes altogether depending on the height at which it was laid, and for only 2 minutes at any one height.

It was obviously of great importance to ensure that no minefield was laid where it might be a danger to friendly aircraft, and Sector Controllers were required to keep all aircraft under their own or G.C.I. control away from air-mining aircraft, but only when the air-mining became a potential danger to them.

Consequently it was necessary that regular and accurate plots of air-mining aircraft should appear on the Operations Tables of Sectors concerned. The actual release of the mine-curtain, which descended at about 1000 feet a minute, was required to be plotted at once in all Sectors concerned.

The G.C.I. station, in whose area the minefield was to be laid, would, from the time the actual interception was initiated, pass plots of the position of the air-mining aircraft to the Sector Operations Room. These plots, under a special designation, were to be repeated to an appropriate Observer Centre by means of the liaison line. Use would then be made of the Observer Corps multiphones to reproduce those plots on the Operations Rooms Tables of the sectors and group to which that Centre reported.

The Inland Reporting Scheme

Before proceeding to a study of the year 1942, it is necessary to consider in some detail the reporting system and proposed changes thereto, as these matters were the subject of innumerable conferences from 1941 onwards throughout the whole course of the war.

It was on July 20th 1941, that the Operational Research Section of Fighter Command produced a report which presented a general survey of the existing reporting methods and specified the function of a practical reporting system. The report also made broad recommendations concerning the future use of reporting instruments, and the reporting system to be used in conjunction with these instruments. It was at this point that the Inland Reporting Scheme originated, a scheme which was never completed in its entirety, but which formed the broad basis from which was evolved the reporting system as it was at the close of the war.

The reporting system had given vital service despite its inherent weakness. The R.D.F. side, comprising the CH and CH. L Stations possessed two main weaknesses:

(i) The difficulty of reporting the very large number of aircraft likely to be involved at any one time.

(ii) A filtering organisation that had not kept pace with the rapid technical improvements at R.D.F. Station.

Over land the Royal Observer Corps was the only organisation that attempted to present the general picture that was demanded by a reporting system. The discrepancies between the reported and the true picture depended directly on the efficiency of human eyes and ears, which, in turn, depended on weather conditions and, to a lesser extent, on the skill of the personnel concerned. It was concluded, therefore, that, the efficiency of the overland reporting system being variable, some supplementary instrument should be provided if a more reliable and complete system was required.

The three instruments available for reporting the movements of aircraft overland were G.L. (Gunlaying), S.L.C. (Searchlight Control), and G.C.I. (Ground Control Interception). Neither of the first two was able to handle more than one track at a time, and, therefore, though they could produce accurate information on selected tracks and were of value for the purposes of interception, they were useless as reporting instruments. G.C.I., on the other hand, though an interception instrument, was ideally suited for reporting and, by various additions, could be used for that purpose without interfering with its primary function.

It was considered that G.C.I. Stations, suitably equipped for reporting, should become the basis of overland reporting, and that their use would facilitate the "Hand-over" between the sea and land reporting systems. In addition, their information was sufficiently accurate to form the limited picture with negligible time-lag, in fact the type of picture needed by Sector Operations and the local Air Raid Warning system. The Royal Observer Corps would be used to fill in the gaps, in the G.C.I. picture, and their information was sufficiently accurate to provide the instantaneous limited picture which was also required.

A complete general picture with a small time-lag could be tolerated by the following organisations which required information in the movement of aircraft:

(i) Fighter Command Operations Room.
(ii) Fighter Group Operations' Rooms.
(iii) The General Air Raid Warning System.
(iv) A.A. Command Organisation.
(v) Under certain circumstances Coastal Command, Naval Operations and Home Defence.

The R.D.F. reporting system needed to be improved by the devolution of filtering groups (this had been commenced), and by the provision of separate lines to each source of information.

The report then went on to consider two methods, by either of which the existing overland reporting system would be improved appreciably. In the first method it was suggested that R.O.C. Centre should be used as collecting points for information, with R.D.F. and G.C.I. plots over the sea displayed on a separate screen, G.C.I. being used thus to assist in the "hand-over" of tracks from the oversea to the overland reporting system. The main distribution of overland information would be either by retelling from the Group Operations Table or, if more desirable, from the Observer Centre itself by extended teleprinter channels.

The second suggested method (and the one which was eventually adopted as a basic principle) was to use inland Filter Rooms as collecting points, thus bringing the inland reporting system into line with the oversea reporting system. The R.O.C. Centres and G.C.I. Stations would have separate lines to plotters at the Inland Filter Room, and G.C.I. information would be monitored at the appropriate R.O.C. Centre. D/X fixes of friendly fighters would be displayed on a separate table in the Inland Filter Room, and R.D.F. and G.C.I. plots over the sea would also be displayed on a separate screen. The correlation of information would be done at the Inland Filter Room, and inter-centre liaison lines would be unnecessary. The great disadvantages in this second system was the unequal time-lag associated with R.O.C. and G.C.I. information.

In conclusion the report suggested that earnest consideration should be given to the matter and that some action should be initiated at an early date.

This question was considered in detail at a conference which took place at Headquarters Fighter Command on March 16th and 17th 1942. It is proposed, therefore, to describe the course of the war during 1942 before further consideration of the Inland Reporting Scheme.

Chapter 7

January 1942 to December 1942

Apart from raids, which were retaliatory for the heavy British bomber offensive, the enemy activity was on similar lines to that pertaining to the latter half of 1941. The retaliatory raids fall into four classes:

(i) The early "Baedeker" raids from April 25th/26th to May 8th/9th.

(ii) Later "Baedeker" raids and other area attacks made from the middle of May onwards.

(iii) Daylight "tip-and-run" raids by fighters and by fighter-bombers.

(iv) Daylight raids by twin-engine aircraft.

Despite the fact that the weight of bombs dropped during the year was only equivalent to that dropped during one month's bombing in the 1940-1941 "blitz" period, the enemy achieved a considerable measure of success for reasons which will appear later in this account.

The "Baedeker" Raids
For the first three months of 1942, the enemy activity was negligible apart from a dusk attack on Portland by about 12 Ju.88s and about 12 fighters, and a sharp night attack on Dover by 10 Do.217s on March 23rd. Occasional attacks were also made during March, on towns and ports on the East coast. Then, after heavy attacks by us on Lübeck and Rostock, enemy activity increased in late April and, as a prelude to the "Baedeker" raids,

a scattered attack on the Exmouth region with some bombs on Exeter, took place on April 23rd/24th. This was followed the next night by an attack on Exeter by about 25 aircraft, bombing from heights of 5,000 to 15,000 feet.

On the following night Bath and Bristol were attacked, the former city, which had no balloon barrage, was bombed from very low altitudes, and suffered severely. Again, on April 26th/27th, these two cities were bombed. This success was followed by attacks on Norwich April 27th/28th, 29th/30th, and May 8th/9th; York on April 28th/29th, Exeter on May 3rd/4th, and Cowes on May 4th/5th.

A very good bombing concentration was recorded in these raids. The main reasons may be summarized as follows:

(i)   Except for the last (and unsuccessful) attack on Norwich, they were made in moonlight and in conditions of good visibility.
(ii) With the above exception (and also that of the in-effective Bristol raid) absence of balloon barrages and paucity of A.A. defences made low altitude bombing possible.
(iii) Fires spread quickly, owing to narrow streets and shops filled with inflammable materials.

In the later "Baedeker" raids, at the end of May and the beginning of June, other types of targets were also attacked. During this period attacks were made on Hull, Poole (twice), Grimsby, Canterbury (thrice), and Ipswich. But in these raids the only attack comparable in raiding efficiency with the previous attacks was that made on Canterbury on the first time, May 31st/June 1st. the fall in efficiency was due to various reasons, the provision of balloon barrages in some cases, decoy fires, and heath fires started by early misplaced incendiaries.

In the next moon period, late June, the enemy lost about 8% of the aircraft employed, and the raids were not very effective, the targets being Southampton (which was strongly defended), Birmingham (and in this case the raid was a complete failure, though Nuneaton suffered considerably) Norwich (now provided with a balloon barrage) and Weston-super-Mare (which was twice raided, comparatively lightly).

In July, when Middlesbrough was once raided, and Birmingham three times, the enemy's battle losses rose to 13%, one of the Birmingham raids being the biggest force employed since the first raid on Bath.

After July, intensive attacks were abandoned, though Canterbury was attacked on the night October 31st/November 1st with losses to the enemy of 15% of the aircraft reaching the city.

The Baedeker Raids – Norwich

Some points of interest, from the Royal Observer Corps' angle, emerge from a study of the early "Baedeker" raids on Norwich. In the report of the first night's activity, on April 27th/28th, it appears that at 23.15 hours the attack opened by the enemy dropping flares and incendiaries and was continued until 0045 hours by other aircraft dropping high explosive bombs. The sea plotting was not very helpful. Tracks appeared well out to sea but as they approached the coast the system appeared to break down and it was necessary for the Centre to allot 13 "N" (local designation) numbers. The enemy aircraft approached the target from the N.N.E., passed west of the city, and made their attack from south-west to north-east.

They all approached at considerable height, probably over 5,000 feet, but dived to the attack, and were frequently very low over the target.

The system of plotting by "Battle Zone" was instituted at 0003 hours as it was no longer possible to distinguish individual tracks. The average height was given as 10,000 feet, but this was probably incorrect as it represented the height given by the last post. The enemy aircraft descended rapidly, but as there was no R.O.C. Post in Norwich itself, it was not possible to be very accurate. At 0025 hours a "Small Zone" was substituted for the "Large Zone" with a maximum of 10 aircraft at an average height of 2,000 feet. This Small Zone was removed at 0048 hours and normal telling was resumed.

Fighters were, as far as possible, told to all Sectors, but it was difficult to say the number operating, though at midnight there were five Beaufighters and two Whirlwinds in the Battle Zone.

On the following night April 29th/30th, very shortly after the introduction of a large Battle Zone, all lines except for two Post

Clusters were put out of action owing to a main cable between the Centre and the Telephone Exchange being severed by a direct hit. Improvised circuits were secured in the early morning but, owing to a further fault developing, it became necessary on the following day to move to the Emergency Centre.

On the third attack, May 8th/9th, the hostile aircraft were flying much higher (a balloon barrage having been provided). There was no moon, but the night was clear and star-lit. Fortunately a flare dropped by an early raider started a fire near a decoy site east of the city, and 5/6ths of the total bomb load was dropped near this fire, in some cases from as low as 800 feet. On this occasion only two of the Observer Posts were out of action.

What was noticeable in all these raids was the difficulty of Centres reporting heights of hostile and of friendly aircraft in the Battle Zone. Sectors naturally required heights estimated as accurately as possible, but heights varied continuously from 10,000 feet to zero during dive-bombing.

The Norwich Centre performed their duties very efficiently during these raids, and the following message was sent to them by the A.O.C.-in-C., Fighter Command, "Please congratulate the members of the Norwich Centre on the efficient manner in which they have carried out their duties during the recent attacks on the City. I am very glad to know that, apart from one minor injury, there have been no casualties among members of the Centre crew".

The "Baedeker" Raids – York

One unfortunate aspect of the raid on York was the delay in giving the public alarm, which was not sounded until after the first bomb had fallen. This caused detrimental comment upon the work of the Royal Observer Corps by uninformed members of the public who, as usual, considered the Corps responsible for alarms being given. The Regional Alarm had been given by the Alarm Controller at least seven minutes before the signal was sounded. The preceding comments are taken from the report of the Duty Controller in Observer Centre Number 9, which, it will be remembered, shared a building with Number 10 centre.

The attack was a heavy one, and various buildings in the immediate vicinity of the Centre were burned out. In addition numerous high explosive bombs fell in close proximity to the Centre building, while three incendiary bombs hit the Centre itself, fortunately in positions where they were easily accessible. The crews of both Observer Centres worked with commendable coolness and efficiency, and they were able to keep contact with the Posts immediately concerned in the raid. They were thus enabled to supply information to Fighter Groups and Sectors, although their teleprinters went out of action and they had to revert to speech-telling. The teleprinters were affected by the vibration caused when a high explosive bomb, dropped near the centre, lifted the machine from the floor.

As a result of this raid, action was taken to requisition land on the outskirts of York on which to build two Standard Centres, though the priority of tis building had yet to be decided. It was realised, however, that despite the advantages of proximity to Telephone Exchanges, the centre of a city was not the best place in which to site an Observer Centre.

The "Baedeker" Raids – Exeter

During the raid on the night of May 3rd/4th, the Observer Centre was damaged by incendiaries and by the water used in putting out fires, and the Emergency Centre was completely destroyed. Great damage was done to the centre of the city, and it was only the strenuous efforts of the crew on duty that saved the Observer centre itself. The Commandant of the Western Area, Royal Observer Corps, arrived at Exeter on the morning of May 4th, and with considerable difficulty succeeded in making arrangements with the City Council for the use as an emergency centre of a store in the cliff side bordering the River Exe. In his report to the Commandant of the Royal Observer Corps he gave it as his opinion that it would be wise to leave the centre of the city and establish an Observer Centre on the outskirts, while retaining the original centre as an Emergency Centre. He also suggested the provision of a third alternative Centre to be used in the event of the destruction of the other two.

To sum up, these early "Baedeker" raids showed the importance of the static and passive elements in a defensive system. It was the absence of balloon barrages, A.A. defences, adequately protected communications and many other requisites that enabled the enemy to cause such confusion and to achieve his not inconsiderable success. It was, of course, not possible, in the then existing state of supplies, to provide adequate defences for every possible target, but the gradual deterioration in the raiding efficiency of the enemy was due to such steps as were taken, coupled with the increasing efficiency of the night fighter technique.

Daylight Tip-and-Run Raids
Preliminary raids of this type had taken place on Christmas Day 1941, when buildings at Fairlight were attacked, and again on the following day, when these raiders were recognised as Me.109. In January and March 1942 similar raids took place, and towards the end of March 1942 attacks were made on Channel shipping and on south coast harbours by Me.109s with bombs. In April, fighter and fighter-bomber attacks intensified, certain specific targets being preferred. These attacks persisted right through the year until in November and December the Mediterranean theatre of operations took precedence, and like the night activity, daylight operations dwindled away. Only one fighter-bomber attack on a land target took place in November, though there were a number of fighter attacks on railway targets. In the middle of December, when the enemy had ceased to fear an imminent invasion of Southern France, fighter bomber attacks were resumed as a regular feature of enemy activity.

The customary tactics in these raids involved the use of Me.109 and of F.W.190 aircraft in pairs or fours, with occasionally larger formations, notably in two fairly big attacks on Hastings and on Canterbury in September and October respectively.

In the attack on Hastings some 20 fighter aircraft, some with bombs, were employed, with a rear cover of 15 to 20 aircraft over the Channel. Encouraged by the comparative cheapness and success of this type of raid, Canterbury was chosen as the next target, in which attack some 60 enemy aircraft were probably used. Of the 44 bombs dropped 31 fell in the target area. This attack was followed by two small bomber raids on Canterbury by night.

Interception of Low Flying Enemy Aircraft
In view of the persistent attacks made by the enemy using very low flying aircraft on coastal targets along the South Coast of

England, various methods were tried to facilitate interception. The difficulties were great as, in view of the low altitude, R.D.F. information was seriously limited, with the result that A.A. defences were frequently unable to come into action until the attack had been delivered. The details of the measures taken to overcome this difficulty are not relevant to this narrative, but in broad outline, involved the provision of C.H.L. information to the appropriate Gun Operations Rooms.

For the same reason measures were taken to accelerate the provision of Royal Observer Corps information in order to attempt the interception of these low flying raiders by our fighter aircraft. This operation, known by the code name of "Totter", involved the issue to certain selected Observer Posts and Coastguard Stations of suitable pyrotechnics. The coastal posts to be issued with these rockets were those in the area extending from the North Foreland to Lands' End.

The posts were ordered to fire a rocket as soon as the low flying enemy aircraft were seen, and to continue to fire them while the hostile aircraft remained in the vicinity.

Standing patrols of pairs of aircraft were to be ordered over vulnerable points on the south coast, and the system of "rocket indication" was to be used as an aid to interception by these aircraft.

The Observer Groups affected by this Order were Groups Numbers 1, 2, 3, 21, 22, 20 and the operation came into effect in November 1942.

In addition to this, in order to speed up the reporting of low flying fighter and fighter-bomber raids, an operation known by the code name of "RATS" was devised, by which, on seeing a low flying enemy aircraft, the R.O.C. post was immediately to pass the word "RATS" to the Observer Centre before passing any plot. This was then to be passed immediately by the Sector Controller, such a message having full priority. This would enable fighters to be scrambled or, if already airborne, to be directed before the actual plot was received. Sector Controllers were to have available a map showing the position of Royal Observer Corps Posts in the Sector.

Satellite Posts
Despite these and other measures it was found that, with the existing spacing of Royal Observer Corps Posts, it was possible

for aircraft to fly for appreciable distances over land at very low altitudes without their tracks being maintained with the continuity required for controlled interception by Fighters and for the issue of Air Raid Warnings.

It was accordingly decided to form approximately 150 "Satellite" reporting posts connected by telephone to the nearest R.O.C. Post (which would act as the "Parent" post) or to the nearest Centre.

Thus it would be possible to increase the low coverage within a bolt of 30 miles width on the South Coast and on the East Coast as far North as Dundee, as well as on the coast of Lancashire and Cheshire.

The duty of these "Satellite" Posts would be to report, during hours of daylight, the visual observation of low flying hostile and doubtful aircraft approaching the coast and flying overland, which existing Royal Observer Corps Posts were unable to observe by reason of their topographical position. By this provision of "Satellite" Posts it was hoped to improve the reporting not only of the low flying coastal raids by single-engine enemy aircraft, but also, to some extent, of the twin-engine bombers which had been adopting similar low flying tactics in their attacks on (in most cases) military targets.

It was obvious that, in order to maintain continuity of tracking and to give adequate warning, it was essential to get plots on raiders at the earliest possible moment, and the further a raider penetrated inland unobserved the more difficult proportionately became the problem of quick identification and formation of track.

Complementary to the measure described above had been a survey on all Posts in the country ordered to be made on August 22nd 1942. The type of survey was so ordered as to give the arcs of visibility of aircraft at 100, 500 and 1500 feet above the ground level of the Posts.

The results of this survey were collated and combined, and complete coverage diagrams for the R.O.C. Group territories were produced by the Operational Research Section. The measures taken as a consequence of this survey will be described in a review of the following year, 1943, a year in which the low flying problem continued, though with less success.

Daylight Attacks by Twin-Engine Aircraft

The renewal of the daylight offensive against land targets was effected by twin-engine bombers as well as by single-engine fighter bombers. They were, in fact, responsible for about 60% of all the daylight activity commenced in July and continued intensively until October. In most cases single aircraft were used in this form of attack, taking advantage of cloud cover and flying very low.

Fair success was achieved and military targets of one sort or another were generally selected, a review of the year's activity showing that over half the attacks recorded were on military targets. On one day in July, for instance, despite very bad weather, some 30 raids of this type were over the country, and they hit and damaged 4 factories, 2 aerodromes and 4 railway targets listed as key points.

At the end of August and the beginning of September, in addition to these low-flying attacks, about 12 flights were made over England at very high altitude, 30,000 feet to above 40,000 feet, by twin-engine aircraft (mostly Ju.86B) most of which dropped one small bomb.

The attacks by twin-engine bombers during daylight, delivered at low altitude, produced a problem similar to that occasioned by the low-flying coastal attacks, and the measures taken to deal with them were primarily the same.

The satellite posts originated by Fighter Command Operational Instruction No.66/1942, were to be established, when the locality was suitable, at R.A.F. Stations, Searchlight Detachments and Coastguard Stations. Arrangements were to be made between the R.A.F. Station Commander and the Observer Group Officer concerned, and as each Satellite Post came into operation, Headquarters Fighter Command was to be informed.

The Inland Reporting Scheme

As has been previously stated, as a result of O.R.S. report No.224 of July 29th, 1941, a Conference took place at Headquarters, Fighter Command on March 16th and 17th 1942, to discuss the Inland Reporting Scheme in detail. The Chairman outlined the objects of the Meeting, dividing them into two main parts, the Inland Reporting System itself and Sub-Stratosphere Interception.

Part I. Inland Reporting System

It was agreed that the increasing heights at which aircraft were flying necessitated the use of all suitable forms of R.D.F. as part of the Raid Reporting System, and, for purposes of over land reporting, it was decided to use Inland G.C.I. Stations. The use of these Stations involved the provision of centres at which information could be collated from all sources, for purposes of filtering and re-telling to the Operations Rooms which needed such information. The most suitable centres for such a purpose appeared to be Fighter Group Filter Rooms.

Human observers reporting all aircraft that they could see or hear would remain an essential part of the Raid Reporting System, not only because Inland R.D.F. could not at that time read aircraft below a height of 6,000 feet, but also for purposes of recognition by visual means, and as a safeguard against "jamming" of our inland R.D.F. Stations.

In the opinion of the Conference, while Combined R.D.F. and R.O.C. information would be required by Command, Group and Sector Operations Rooms, Sector Operations Rooms would need, in addition, R.O.C. information covering the Sector Area to be told direct to them.

It was not considered that R.O.C. Centres would require raid information from Inland and Coastal R.D.F. Stations, but that liaison lines would be necessary between R.O.C. Centres and Inland R.D.F. Stations in order to facilitate recognition and thus eliminate, as far as possible, congestion in the Reporting System. R.O.C. Centres would receive information from their own Posts, but would only liaise with Inland R.D.F. Stations, and with Fighter Group Filter Rooms where their R.O.C. Liaison Officers would now be situated.

With regard to the reporting of friendly fighter aircraft, it was decided that provision should be made, in the revised Reporting System, for "plots" of fighter aircraft to be told inwards from each Sector to its Group Filter Room, and thence outwards to all Operations Rooms and to adjacent Group Filter Rooms concerned.

Part II. Sub-Stratosphere Interceptions

In connection with the interception of sub-stratosphere raiders the speed and heights of these aircraft, and the time taken for our fighters to attain the necessary height for interception, made it essential for the initial patrol orders to be given to groups by Command, the Duty Air Commodore being the controlling authority, and basing his decisions on Coastal R.D.F. information.

The action would then devolve upon the Group or Groups selected, making use of information from R.D.F., G.C.I., and R.O.C. sources, such information being collated on a specialised form of "Interception Table" devised and fitted in each Group Filter Room. The initial order having been given by Command on Coastal R.D.F. plots, it was not necessary for G.C.I. Stations to tell direct to Command, but it would suffice for G.C.I. information to be retold to Command from Group Filter Rooms.

These policy decisions were conveyed to the Headquarters of all the Fighter Groups, and they were at the same time asked to consider the problems arising therefrom, and to give their views on the various questions involved as they affected each individual group. A small Filter Room Planning Committee was to be set up at Headquarters Fighter Command to which Group representatives would be invited.

Change of Commandant, Royal Observer Corps
The whole question of inland reporting, in so far as it affected the Royal Observer Corps, is intimately concerned with the changes instituted by the Commandant in the internal arrangements and procedure of the Corps. These changes were the result of a change of Commandant which took place on June 25th 1942. Air Commodore Warrington-Morris, who had commanded the Corps for over six years, was succeeded by Air Commodore G.H. Ambler, O.B.E., A.F.C., a serving officer of the Royal Air Force, who brought to bear on the problems of the Royal Observer Corps a brain highly trained in operational matters and methods.

Inter-Centre Hand-over of Tracks
In a letter to Area Commandants in which he gave a brief description of the proposed changes in the Inland Reporting System, the Commandant, Royal Observer Corps, also described a project with which the scheme was intimately connected. This

was an attempted solution of one of the most consistent faults in the Royal Observer Corps reporting, namely the handing over of tracks between Centres. As he said, this was at present covered only by the Inter-Centre Tellers, the method was crude, and was liable to break down seriously, particularly at night. It was considered that most of the complaints that were received of lack of continuity in R.O.C. tracking in cases where aircraft were flying over several R.O.C. Groups could be accounted for by faulty hand-over, though it was admitted that it was frequently difficult for Posts to plot specified aircraft through training areas.

Out of three Schemes submitted by Headquarters, Royal Observer Corps, to Fighter Command, to deal with this difficult question, and coupled with the Inland Reporting problem, the plan known as "Modified Lateral Scheme 'B'" had been accepted. Application for an increased establishment for Centre Crews required for this new Scheme were being submitted to the Air Ministry.

It may be mentioned, in passing, that the need for increased establishments eventually proved to be a stumbling block and a cause of considerable modification in the Inland Reporting Scheme as a whole, particularly as the demand came at a time of acute shortage both of man and woman power.

Modified Lateral Scheme "B"

In the introductory paragraphs to his description of this scheme the Commandant mentioned that, with a view to assisting in identification of incoming tracks, 10 G.L. Sets were to be deployed between Flamborough Head and Shoeburyness in order to identify I.F.F. Interrogation. This scheme was being implemented in an attempt to sort out enemy aircraft, particularly of the intruder type, from our returning bombers.

The successful employment of G.L. Sets would, however, prove of little worth unless continuous tracks could be produced by the R.O.C., following G.L. identification. Also lack of continuous tracking caused a duplication of tracks with the result that more enemy aircraft were shown on Operations Rooms Tables than actually existed in the air. This, again, resulted in wasted effort on the part of the active defences.

Track Displays

In each R.O.C. Centre there was to be provided a large vertical sheet-iron plotting map fixed on a stand in such a way that 9 plotters could be comfortably seated round it.

The area covered by this map was to be that of the Centre Table with a margin of 30 miles all round it, and the scale of the map was to be half the scale of the main plotting table.

Plotting was to be by the use of magnetic plotting symbols, in order that it should be possible to plot on the vertical map as if it were horizontal.

Inter-Centre Passing of Plots

The existing two-directional lateral circuits between Centres were to be split to become two uni-directional circuits in opposite directions. Additional Inter-Centre Tellers were to be provided on a scale to allow of not more than three outgoing circuits to each Teller. The incoming circuits from adjacent Centres were to terminate on jacks around the edge of the vertical plotting map.

The Inter-Centre Tellers would then tell outgoing tracks from their Centre to the adjacent centres affected, both hostile and friendly tracks being told in this way.

Plotters on the vertical plotting map would then plot the tracks received on to the vertical plotting map.

Taking Over Tracks in a Centre

The Duty Controller's Assistant would be the person responsible in each Centre for the taking over of tracks of aircraft flying into the area covered by his Centre. He was to be so positioned that he could see the vertical plotting map, and thus give warning to the Posts or the Post Plotters of any incoming tracks, for this purpose making use of the monitoring keyboard already provided.

As soon as a track on the vertical plotting map was picked up and plotted on the main plotting table, the raid plaque was to be transferred from the vertical plotting map to the main plotting table.

It is not intended to go more fully, at this point, into the details of the Inland Reporting Scheme, as, by January 1943, the decision had been taken to postpone the Scheme indefinitely. In fact, at a later stage, the project was revived and, in a modified form, a large number of the policy decisions were implemented.

The changes in the handing over of tracks between Observer Centres, involving the provision of a belt of cover of 30 miles round each Centre area, were of major importance, as they made possible the decentralization of Air Raid Warnings, the story of which will be described in an account of the year 1943.

Use of G.L. Equipment by the R.O.C. for Identification of Sound-Plots

In their Report No.328, the Operational Research Section, Fighter Command, proposed that G.L. Sets should be provided for use in conjunction with R.O.C. Centres. The reason given for this suggestion was that, once aircraft were over the coast, coming inland, apart from recognition by G.C.I. Stations of those aircraft carrying I.F.F. Mark IIG there was no positive means of identification except recognition by sight. The use of G.L. Sets, to be used as an identification aid, for interrogation and not for tracking, would enable the Royal Observer Corps to eliminate plots that would otherwise need to be tracked as unidentified or hostile. It might, indeed, prove possible, by a process of elimination, to identify positively hostile aircraft on intruder missions to this country.

At a conference held at Headquarters, Fighter Command on August 6th 1942, it was agreed, after discussion, to recommend to the A.O.C.-in-C., that A.A. Command should be requested to take the necessary steps with regard to siting, provision of G.L. Sets and of personnel necessary for maintenance.

Various difficulties arose in connection with the provision of the necessary telephone circuits and, eventually, it was decided the 10 G.L. Sets which were to be used should be sited at existing R.O.C. posts, and that the sets should be in operation during the hours of darkness, during which time the Post concerned would close down, the telephone line from the Post to the Centre being used by the crew of the G.L. Set. In Operations Procedure Order No.46 it was stated that the 10 G.L. Sets were to be deployed to cover the coast line of the following R.O.C. Centres: York (No. 10 R.O.C. Group), Lincoln, Colchester – two sets each, Norwich – 3 sets, Bury St. Edmunds – 1 set.

At each R.O.C. Centre concerned a member, known as the Interrogator, was to read unidentified plots appearing on the

R.O.C. table to the G.L. Set in whose area the aircraft was flying. The G.L. Operator would then check whether or not the aircraft was showing I.F.F.

Immediately the Duty Controller in the R.O.C. Centre was satisfied that a track identified previously as "Hostile" or "X" (i.e. doubtful) represented, in fact an aircraft positively showing I.F.F. he was, on his own authority, to change the raid designation to "friendly".

This information, passed through by the R.O.C. Tellers, was to be shown in Operations Rooms, by the display, alongside the raid block, of the I.F.F. Square as used by Filterers in Group Filter Rooms.

This procedure came into effect on November 13th 1942. In a revision of the Procedure Order at the end of the year, the G.L. Interrogator, in the R.O.C. Centre, was instructed to select plots for interrogation in the following order of preference:- (1) Hostile, (2) Unidentified, (3) Friendly sea tracks, (4) Friendly land tracks. In response to the Interrogator's enquiries the G.L. Operator would state that the plot was either 'not seen', 'unidentified', 'friendly' or 'S.O.S.' A distinction was also made between the action to be taken by the Duty Controller at the Centre with reference to R.D.F. and R.O.C. tracks whose designation was shown, by G.L. interrogation, to be inaccurate.

Tracks which showed broad I.F.F. were to be labelled S.O.S., in the case of R.D.F. tracks the information being, of course, passed to the Filter Room Controller by the R.O.C. Liaison Officer in the Fighter Group Operations Room.

Report on Results of G.L. Interrogation
A report rendered on February 23rd 1943, showed that, over a period of 6 weeks more than 8,500 aircraft had been challenged by this means, and the results may be summarized as follows:

Number of occasions G.L. Sets were responsible for changing "X" to "Friendly" tracks – 21.

Number of occasions G.L. Sets were responsible for preventing double tracking of aircraft – 14.

Number of occasions G.L. Sets picked up tracks of aircraft showing S.O.S. – 10.

It was recommended in the report that public wire circuits

should be utilized to provide connections between G.L. Equipment and R.O.C. Centres, thus obviating delay in the passing of plots from the other posts in the cluster. It had been found that great difficulty was experienced by other Posts on the same cluster as a G.L. Interrogator was working, and that this had on occasions delayed the plots of hostile aircraft.

This request for special circuits between the G.L. Sets and the appropriate Royal Observer Corps Centres was approved by the Air Ministry on March 30th 1943.

Chapter 8

January 1943 to December 1943

During the course of the year 1943, though the tonnage of bombs dropped on these islands was only about one half of that dropped during 1942, an attempt was made to compensate for this by increased accuracy. Faster aircraft were used and by mingling with the stream of returning British Bombers, it was probably hoped to reduce losses.

Events in the Mediterranean theatre of operations stopped attempts on the part of the enemy to build up a large striking force of fighter-bombers for use against Great Britain, and, in fact, during the last three months of the year under review, flights over this country by enemy aircraft of any kind were rare.

The Night Offensive

The first intensive night raid for nearly six months (apart from the two-wave attack on Canterbury in October 1942) was made on London by about 75 long-range bombers on January 17th/18th, but of these aircraft only 15 reached London and 11% of the total were destroyed.

During the first three months of the year attacks were made against Swansea, London, Southampton, Newcastle, Hull, Sunderland, Grimsby, Norwich, Yarmouth, Edinburgh and Hartlepool, in all cases with negligible success, and with a considerable percentage of loss in many cases.

Meanwhile our bomber offensive was growing and American bombers were appearing over German cities, and in March 1943, Hitler appointed an officer known as the "Augriffsfuhrer England", to take charge of bombing operations against this country. Changes were noticeable almost immediately. Firstly, in April fighter-bombers at heights up to 30,000 feet were used against London by moonlight. Their speed made them difficult to shoot down, though 3 of these aircraft, lost and short of fuel, landed at West Malling, thinking they were on their own side of the Channel. Next, in the same month, an attack by about 30 long-range bombers was made on Aberdeen (which was not provided with a balloon barrage) from a low altitude.

During May and June fighter-bomber attacks with forces of moderate size were made against London (five times), Norwich, Sunderland (twice), Cardiff, Chelmsford, Plymouth, Grimsby and Hull. During some of these raids marker flares were used, and during the Grimsby raid a large number of anti-personnel bombs were dropped, with considerable effect among the public.

During June the enemy used Me. 410 light bombers in nuisance raids on this country, and on all three nights on which they were used, they succeeded in getting over this country without being recognised as hostile, and none were shot down. While there were two successful raids on Grimsby and Hull in July and nuisance raids by Me. 410, in the following month there was a distinct decline in performance and the enemy casualties rose sharply. This was despite the fact that in raids on Plymouth and on Lincoln, in August, Pathfinder methods were said by the enemy to have been used, including the placing by picked crews of turning-point and target-indicator flares.

During August also there was a recrudescence of intruder activity, a new unit equipped with Me.410 coming into action. There was considerable use of anti-personnel bombs, and there were nineteen nocturnal raids on aerodromes.

In September intruder and nuisance raids continued, and in October there were four relatively concentrated raids, of which the only one at all successful was on London on the night of October 7th/8th. In the last two months of the year activity was very slight.

The Day Offensive

The long-range bomber activity in daylight never rose to the level reached in the summer and early autumn of 1942, and after the end of February was very slight. In the last three months of the year 1943, only 10 enemy aircraft of all types are known to have flown over the United Kingdom in daylight, and three of these were destroyed.

On the other hand, for the first three months of the year, the position with regard to enemy fighter-bomber activity was not satisfactory. Many minor attacks were made by aircraft in small formations with, occasionally, more ambitious attacks by formations of between 12 and 30 fighter bombers with or without an escort and rear cover. In January 12 fighter-bombers bombed the crowded areas round Poplar and Bermondsey from low altitudes with considerable moral effect. This was followed by several other similar attacks, on Eastbourne, Hastings, London and Ashford, among other places.

The problem was to get adequate warning of these low flying raids as, though enemy casualties were high, these casualties mostly took place after the bombs had been dropped. The use of Radar equipment involving low coverage was tried in spring and early summer, and with some success.

After March attacks were almost entirely confined to coastal towns, and few of the towns along the south and east coats, from Torquay to Yarmouth were without experience of this type of raid. At the end of the first week in June these tip-and-run raids ceased. Undoubtedly the enemy had found it increasingly dangerous to make daylight sorties over this country, and in addition, with the successful conclusion of the Tunisian campaign, units were transferred to the Mediterranean area.

There is little doubt that, in any case, we had, by the end of the year, attained air supremacy over this country.

Measures to Combat the Tip-and-Run Raids

As has been previously mentioned, from a survey of the siting of all R.O.C. posts made in August 1942, coverage diagrams were prepared and, based on these various suggestions were put forward by the Commandant in a letter to Headquarters, Fighter Command in February 12th 1943. Horizontal visibility was assessed as follows:

An aircraft at 100 feet – 2 miles
An aircraft at 500 feet – 4 miles
An aircraft at 1500 feet – 6 miles

These figures were fixed according to the possibility of recognising an aircraft by type, and also on the grounds that the higher the aircraft was the more likely it would be for it to be visible against the background of sky.

Working on the coverage diagrams of the four Observer Groups most intimately concerned with the entrance of low-flying raiders into this country, i.e. Maidstone, Horsham, Winchester and Bromley, it appeared that there were many gaps in the R.O.C. coverage at 100 feet above ground level, along the coast. There were also several 'blind alleys', along which it was possible for aircraft to fly in as far as the Thames, at heights up to 500 feet above ground level without being spotted by any R.O.C. Post.

Against this there were certain Coastguard Stations linked by a direct line to an R.O.C. Post, and these Coastguard Stations did apparently fill some of the Coastal gaps. They were, on the other hand, manned by Coastguards not highly trained in aircraft recognition, and to whom aircraft observation was, in fact, a secondary function. Also, as the lines were terminated at the R.O.C. Post, reports had to be relayed to the Observer Centre, the delay thus caused detracting from the value of the report.

In making his recommendations as to methods of combating low flying raiders, the Commandant used the following premises as a foundation for his suggestions:

(ii)   That all aircraft crossing the coast at heights down to 100 feet must be seen in order that the 'Rats' warning might be given to all forms of defence.

(ii)   That inland from the coast there should be no 'blind alleys' at 100 feet on a straight line longer than, say, 12 miles.

(iii) That inland from the coast there should be no 'blind alleys' at 100 feet longer than 12 miles in the form of a line following some natural feature or contour (e.g. railway, river or valley).

His recommendations, which were of considerable value, may be given in detail:

(a) The apparent 'cover' afforded by 28 selected Coastguard Stations combined with the existing R.O.C. coastal posts would give, in condition of 2 miles or greater horizontal visibility, an un-interrupted ring of cover down to 100 feet height from Chatham to Portsmouth.

(b) It was suggested, therefore, that a survey should be made of those selected Coastguard Stations on the lines of the R.O.C. Visibility Charts.

(c) If this proved satisfactory, the Coastguard Stations should be provided with the normal communication to Centres, should, in fact, be made one of a 'Cluster' of Posts connected on an omnibus circuit to a Plotter at the R.O.C. Observer Centre Operations Room Table. 'Cluster' consisting of four Posts (3 Coastal and 1 Inland) could be provided to cover the coastline of the Horsham and Maidstone R.O.C. Groups, and in the case of Maidstone this would necessitate the formation of 3 new 'Clusters', with 3 new lines terminating at the Centre. In the case of Horsham, by increasing the present 3 Post Clusters to 4 Post Clusters, no new formations would be required.

(d) Each selected and connected Coastguard Station should be manned by one R.O.C. Observer, in addition to the Coastguard, during the daylight hours, and, though this would involve a manning problem of considerable magnitude, the problem was not insuperable.

(e) 17 'Clusters' would cover the coast from Chatham to Portsmouth. A push button in one Post per Cluster would serve to give an immediate Air Raid Warning to nearby towns in the case of a hostile aircraft being seen by any Post in the Cluster. Push buttons with connections to L.A.A. batteries could be similarly operated.

The above measures were intended to deal with the provision of additional coastal cover, while to improve inland cover by the eradication of the 'blind alleys' would be a relatively simple matter, involving the re-siting of existing Posts.

In his opinion, though these recommendations called for considerable manning and communications requirements, they represented the only satisfactory method of reporting low flying enemy aircraft. In order to complete the alterations within reasonable time, high Air Ministry priority would be needed.

Owing to the urgency of the question of dealing with this form of enemy attack, steps were taken immediately to implement the proposals put forward by the Commandant, and, by March 10th, eighteen Coastguard Stations were chosen in the Maidstone Observer Corps Area and ten in the area of the Horsham Group. It was found that 77 additional personnel were needed to provide the necessary Observers for these Coastguard Posts, and that a sight alteration was needed in the boundary between Horsham and Maidstone so as to avoid over-crowding the Maidstone Centre Operations Table.

The position, as described at a Conference at Headquarters R.O.C., on April 29th 1943, was that the regrouping in the Maidstone and Horsham R.O.C. Groups was due to commence on May 14th and completion was expected by May 20th. Detailed investigation, by the G.P.O. of the Winchester, Yeovil and Exeter Groups had not yet been completed, but a rough estimate for completion was July 31st.

By the end of May the coast had been covered from the Thames Estuary as far as Selsey Bill, but by the end of the first week in June the tip-and-run raids ceased, though, despite this, it was decided in August to extend the use of Coastguard Stations to the East Coast and to continue the chain as far as the Wash.

Summary
The action taken to meet the menace of tip-and-run raiders and of low flying enemy aircraft generally may thus be summarised under the following headings of measures taken from 1941-1943:

(i)   Issue of Rockets to Observer Posts – Operation "Totter".
(ii)   Operation "Rats".
(iii) Standing Patrols of friendly fighters.
(iv)   Satellite Posts.
(v)   Coastguard Posts.
(vi)   Re-siting of existing Posts.
(vii) Direct warnings from Observer Posts.
(viii) Alarm Controllers in Observer Centres.
(ix)   The use of special low-looking Radar.

The combination of all these may be said to have defeated, or, at any rate, to have made unprofitable that particular form of hostile activity.

The Air Raid Warning System

Though the Air Raid Warning System has been mentioned previously in this narrative, the period under review in this Section (1943) is a convenient time at which to discuss the system as a whole as, with the reorganization of the Royal Observer Corps under the new Commandant, a complete change was effected in the distribution of warnings to the country.

An attempt had been made to confine this account to the system in so far as it affected the Royal Observer Corps though, of necessity, in producing a narrative a good deal of detail creeps in with which the Corps was not immediately concerned.

The Radar System, over the sea, and the Observers over land supplied, of course, the information on which warnings were sounded, and it happened, not infrequently, that the general public, with their inadequate knowledge of the defensive system of Great Britain, blamed the Corps when the Air Raid Warning System was not, in their opinion, efficiently operated.

By June 1940 it was beginning to be realised that the Air Raid Warning System should be modified, or appreciably altered, in order to diminish the evil effect on production caused by the interruption both of the work of men on night shifts and of the night's rest of the workers who had been on the day shifts. A conference was convened accordingly, with the Minister of Home Security as chairman, to discuss these matters. The responsibility for the issue of warnings was at that time in the hands of Headquarters, Fighter Command, and Air Chief Marshal Sir Hugh Dowding was therefore present at this conference. He pointed out that the system was essentially flexible and that warnings could be issued or withheld as required.

Probably owing to the extreme centralization of the system at that time, the decisions of the conference were inconclusive. The Minister, in summing up, said that if any alteration were to be made in the warning system it appeared to be essential that there should be a Public Statement, so that it could be made clear that the responsibility rested with the Government. He was of the opinion that the time had come when a public announcement could be made that the number of warnings would be reduced, coupled with an exhortation to workers in vital industries to carry on after a warning had been given.

It is necessary to show how the main problems with which the Government were confronted in this matter led up to the decentralization of the issue of Air Raid Warnings which eventually involved the Observer Corps. The intention at this time was:

(i)   To introduce a modified warning to have the effect of extinguishing exempted lighting (such as that at railway marshalling yards, docks and shipyards).

(ii) To exhort the workers to remain at their posts.

(iii) Not to arouse the day-shifts or the general public, who were asleep in their houses, by the issue of any warning.

(iv) That the "Red" warning should not be abolished altogether, but should still be sounded at the discretion of the C.-in-C., Fighter Command, if it was found that some target was being approached by large enemy air forces and was likely to be the object of heavy attack.

In a letter to the Prime Minister, on June 29th 1940, the Commander-in-Chief, Fighter Command, emphasized the necessity of a public announcement, at the earliest possible moment, telling the general populace what they must expect, and giving the reasons for the action taken. He pointed out that the general public complained that no warning was given to them before the bombs began to fall, (that is to say, if "Red" warnings were withheld) and that the Police and A.R.P. workers similarly complained that they were not given the opportunity of completing the preparations which they normally made on receipt of the "Red" warning. Also, totally undeserved blame was being attributed to the Observer Corps and other organisations, which were of course, entirely guiltless.

As a result of a Report by the Minister of Home Security, based on consultations with the Air Staff and Fighter Command, it was decided at a meeting of the War Cabinet, on July 9th 1940 to introduce a new "Purple" message, to be known as a "Lights

Warning", on receipt of which all exempted external lighting would be extinguished. This warning would be issued to districts in the track of the raiders which were not expected to be the subject of serious or sustained attack, but which might be bombed if exempted lighting were not extinguished. No public warning would be given, provided, of course, that, if this message had not been preceded by the "Yellow" message, all the action normally taken on the latter message, would be taken on the "Purple".

This new procedure came into force on July 25th 1940, and it was also decided to set up a Committee under the Chairmanship of the Home Secretary to review warning arrangements from time to time. This committee contained representatives of the Home Office, the Employers Federation, the T.U.C., and also of the following Government Departments: Ministry of Labour, Admiralty (Production Side), Air Ministry, Ministry of Supply, Ministry of Aircraft Production.

It was on August 2nd 1940 that the first suggestion was made by the Commandant of the Observer Corps that this formation should be connected more intimately with the issue of Air Raid Warnings. This was the first step towards the decentralization that followed subsequently. He suggested that at central points to which warnings were sent by Fighter Command plotting tables of appropriate scale should be installed to cover the existing warning areas plus a calculated area of approach. The plotters should be connected to the necessary number of adjacent Observer Centres and should receive plots of enemy raids simultaneously with Fighter Groups and Sectors.

It should, in his opinion, be the responsibility of the local Air Raid Warning Officer to have the warning sounded in such towns as he might decide, subject to the over-riding control from Fighter Command. By this means the time-lag would be lessened by the sounding of the warning on information received direct from the Observer Centres. Also the shorter the time between the issue of warnings and the arrival of the raiders, the fewer the number of places that it would be necessary to warn.

There was undoubtedly at this time a growing feeling of dissatisfaction among the civilian population regarding the efficiency of the Air Raid Warning System, and this was having its repercussions among the Observer Corps, whose members were frequently assailed by criticism and abuse from their friends and neighbours, under the still prevailing impression that the Corps was responsible for the system and its shortcomings.

The Observer Group Officer of No.16 (Norwich) Observer Group, an area in which dissatisfaction was rampant, had written to the Commandant on August 1st 1940 suggesting that "the remedy seems obvious in the decentralization of the siren system, one which will give adequate reassurance to the general public and one of great encouragement to the Observers... These views have been expressed after the fourth local raid with unfortunately a great number of casualties and on each occasion no warning has been given." He went on to say that all the principle factories in that locality (Norwich) were organising their own Observer look-outs as no longer could any trust be given to that of the sirens.

On August 2nd 1940, the Ministry of Home Security received a deputation from Norwich asking what could be done to give the city better notice of attack by hostile aircraft, and asking for a new and decentralized system. In this case, the situation was becoming serious as the city was in a ferment and Messrs. Boulton and Pauls had decided to suspend production as a result of extensive damage to the Works. In this case it was decided to adopt the use of "Red" warnings on a liberal scale, this procedure to be adopted immediately and to continue for one month. This city was of course in a particularly unfortunate position, being a crowded town with many narrow streets, and being close to the coast, with sea on three sides, could not receive much warning of impending air attack.

As a matter of fact, the raid which had brought the feeling to a head had been made by a captured Blenheim which had been correctly identified as a Blenheim by the Observer Corps but, somewhat naturally, not recognised as hostile.

During the course of the discussion between the Ministry of Home Security and the deputation from the City of Norwich it transpired that, though those in authority in Norwich had every reason to believe that the Observer Corps system was functioning well and passing on information of enemy aircraft spotted, morale in the city was definitely shaken, and stones had been thrown at Observer Corps cars.

At the conference held on August 6th 1940, it was pointed out that the enemy's present tactics were obviously aimed at the maximum dislocation of our production efforts at the minimum cost to himself by covering wide distances but dropping few bombs. For that reason "Red" warnings were being confined to those places which it was expected would be objects of attack. It was an inevitable consequence that some places would be bombed without warning and others warned without bombing.

It was agreed that in places where a "Red" warning had been given every effort should be made to continue work in important factories as far as reasonably possible, and for this reason it might be a useful precaution to arrange between Employers and Employees in each factory to post a watcher on the roof who would sound an alarm within the factory if there were any evidence of approaching attack. The system of roof-watchers, which had already been unofficially started, was now officially sanctioned.

To sum up the situation, those in authority were subjected to considerable complaints, among which the case of the City of Norwich has been taken as only one example among many. As the Commander-in-Chief, Fighter Command said, in his reply to one of such complaints: "Our pre-knowledge of raids is limited by the capacity of science and the power of audition possessed by the human ear (when visual observation is impossible). Over England much enemy flying takes place above the clouds. In the case of machines flying very high it may easily happen that they come down to 20,000 feet and are heard at that height for the first time. The head of the Observer Corps considers that 20,000 feet is the limit of reliable audibility." In his unenviable position, the Commander-in-Chief, had to implement a policy which involved restricting the "Red" warnings and accelerating the "All Clear" in order to satisfy the demands of the War Production Authorities. At the same time he had virtually to guess what the ultimate objective of the enemy pilot might be.

The question of the use of the Observer Corps information more adequately to effect the issue of warnings came more to the fore in September 1940, when the first meeting of the Air Raid Warning Committee took place, presided over by the Assistant Chief of the Air Staff. As a result of this and of a subsequent meeting proposals were made which were approved by the War Cabinet on October 14th 1940. Among these proposals was that an Alarm Controller should be appointed for each Observer Corps Centre. These officers were to be responsible for preparing and administering schemes for the issue of alarms within the area of each Centre.

This was a direct result of the strength and extent of the public demand, especially from those engaged in war production, both employers and employed, for the provision of a reliable secondary warning to be given when the danger of attack on important objectives and centres was imminent. All were fully conscious of the limitations inherent in the simple roof-watchers system.

At a meeting of the War Cabinet the question whether these Alarm Controllers should be appointed by the Ministry of Home Security rather than by the Air Ministry was reserved for further consideration, and it was suggested that on general grounds it would be preferable that one Department should be responsible for the whole of the air raid warning organisation.

The Commander-in-Chief, Fighter Command, on being asked for his opinion, stated that he, personally, could not agree to being made responsible for the operations of the Alarm Controllers. If they were installed in Observer Corps Centres, their work, its results and the correspondence arising therefrom must be the responsibility of the Home Office. He believed that this principle of attempting to warn 'Spots' as opposed to districts, was unsound.

It was in May 1942, that it became necessary to devise some method of adapting the Air Raid Warning System to cope with hit-and-run raids on the South Coast of England. A meeting was held at the Home Office on May 22nd to discuss proposals for combating this menace. It had been found that in a number of cases where the objectives of such raids were towns where the local industrial "Alarm" (by then in full operation) from the Observer Corps Centre was received, the "Alarm" had been in time, while the air raid sirens had been late. Where the enemy, coming in low over the sea, had been undetected by R.D.F. and had made an exact land-fall and had to pass along the coast the local industrial alarm, coming 3 to 4 minutes before the sirens, had been effective.

As the local alarm, however, only passed to a limited number of places along the coast, it was suggested that direct connections should be provided between the Telephone Exchange, which was the District Distributing Centre for the following districts, and the appropriate Observer Corps Centre:

Districts		Observer Corps Centre
Canterbury, Folkestone, Hasting with		Maidstone
Brighton, Worthing	with	Horsham
Portsmouth, Bournemouth	with	Winchester
Weymouth	with	Yeovil
Exeter, Torquay, Plymouth	with	Exeter
Truro, Falmouth	with	Truro
Great Yarmouth	with	Norwich

It was proposed that these lines should terminate in the Observer Corps Centre before the Alarm Controller, and in the District Distributing Centre Exchanges on the incoming trunk board, and be used by the Alarm Controller for injecting an "Air Raid Warning 'Red'" message into the warning system. The Post Office would then distribute this message throughout the warning district unless it had been anticipated by a 'Red' message from the main Distributing Centre.

When this procedure was adopted it would be necessary to inform the appropriate Air Raid Warning Officer at Headquarters in order that he might accept the responsibility for issuing a Release message, as the Alarm Controller at the Observer Centre had not a sufficiently wide picture of the raid position to enable him to do this. In no case was it proposed that the Alarm Controller should issue a "White" message to the District Distributing Centre.

This proposed system was not, by any means, the devolution of the responsibility for the issue of "Red" warnings to the Alarm Controller at the Observer Centre, but was intended to deal with the particular form of enemy attack which was then under consideration.

At the discussion which took place of these proposals it was suggested by the Commandant of the Royal Observer Corps that an improvement would be for Observer Posts to be allowed to send the signal direct to coastal towns in cases where their siting put them in a position favourable for such action to be taken. This would overcome the delay involved in passing plots to the Observer Centre and in passing the message to the District Distributing Centre in cases where the aircraft were obviously hostile. He suggested that the town affected should then advise the District Distributing Centre over the ordinary telephone lines and that the "Red" message should then be passed to the remainder of the Warning District.

This latter idea was obviously open to the objection that, apart from the time this would take, it would be impossible to tell with certainty from whom the call had originated.

It was therefore agreed that the Observer Post should signal the neighbouring town to sound its siren, and should then notify the Observer Centre of the action taken. The Alarm Controller would then pass the same message to the District Distributing Centre for onward transmission to the remainder of the Warning District.

It was agreed that, as that type of low flying raid was being made by day only, these proposals should apply only within daylight hours, when the tally of warnings was not complicated by purple messages. These proposals, having been agreed by the Air Staff, were put into operation at an early date, the district of Colchester being added to the list on October 4th, as the result of bombs being dropped without warning on September 28th and 30th 1942. In fact, on those two occasions the Alarm Controller at Colchester Observer Centre issued the Industrial Alarm, but delayed plotting on the Fighter Command Table caused the public warning to be too late. These two incidents had given rise to unrest amongst the workers in Colchester, who threatened to strike unless the public alarms were sounded whenever the imminent danger alarm was received.

Devolution of National Air Raid Warnings
The industrial alarm scheme had been a direct result of the dislocation to industry caused by the widespread raids in the summer and autumn of 1940, and it proved to be an unqualified success. On May 19th 1943, a Conference of Regional Commissioners was held and, among the items on the Agenda,

was the question of the devolution of National Air Raid Warnings to Royal Observer Corps Centres.

The system of industrial alarms was explained and it was stated that "the success of this scheme has, in one sense, been embarrassing, since the reliability of the 'Alarm' and the confidence which is felt in it have had the effect of discrediting the national air raid warning, more particularly in those coastal areas where the alarm is sounded publicly".

As a result of the re-organisation of the Royal Observer Corps and, in particular the installation of long-range tables (which enabled Centres to receive and plot information of raids in the area covered by adjoining Centres), sufficient information would be available at each Centre to enable national air raid warnings to be issued at their existing range. The information from local Observer Posts would be earlier, and that obtained by radiolocation or told from adjoining Centres would not be later, than the information available at Fighter Group Headquarters from which the warnings were then issued.

Another advantage to be obtained from the proposed scheme was the elimination of the present lack of co-ordination resulting from the issue of warnings by two different agencies. The information which they received was substantially the same, but often differently interpreted. It was proposed, therefore, that the national red, purple, and white messages should, as soon as the re-organisation of the Royal Observer Corps was completed, be given from Centres by the Alarm Controllers who at that time gave industrial alarm signals.

This devolution of warnings was the continuation of the policy of decentralisation which had commenced by the stage in which, in 1941, warnings had been decentralised from Fighter Command to the Fighter Groups. It would lead to economy of staff, as the warning staffs at Fighter Groups would become redundant, and also to greater safety, as the disruption if one Observer Centre were knocked out would be much less than if a Fighter Group were put out of action.

Approval was given by the Cabinet for the decentralization of the issue of National Warnings to Observer Centres and, in the letter in which this fact was communicated to Regional Officers, it was explained that it would be some time before the transfer of responsibility from the Air Ministry to the Ministry of Home Security took place. In fact, it was expected the transfer would start about the end of July, beginning at the same time as the introduction of the new plotting system in Centres and working parallel with the Royal Observer Corps programme. The start would be made with the Truro Centre and proceed thence along the South Coast, then back westwards from Colchester to South Wales, then across again from East Anglia to North Wales, and thereafter to and fro across the northern part of Great Britain, ending with Inverness.

On November 17th 1943, the new system came into force at Truro Observer Centre, and the transfer of responsibility for the issue of National Warnings to the Warning Officers in the remaining Centres was completed according to the original plan, the whole of the English section being finished within some six months.

At 1500 hours on April 14th 1944, the transfer of responsibility was completed, and thereafter warnings throughout England, Wales and Scotland were issued by Ministry of Home Security officials stationed at Royal Observer Corps Centres.

A booklet, known as 'Air Raid Warning Instructions – August 1943', was issued to Warning Officers by the Ministry of Home Security, but details of this are not relevant to this narrative of the Royal Observer Corps, as the Corps was merely responsible for providing the information on which the warnings were issued. Some description of the method in which this information was displayed (in so far as it concerned the Warning Officers) may not, however, be out of place.

In order that Warning Officers might be aware of warnings which had been given to adjacent Warning Districts, arrangements were made for warnings to be 'told' by the R.O.C. Tellers to adjacent Centres.

When a Warning Officer decided to issue a warning message he would, after passing the message to the District Distributing Centre operator, throw a key which lit a lamp of the appropriate colour (red, purple or white) on the Inter-Centre Teller's position, and (red or purple) on a warning display pane above the vertical table. The Inter-Centre Teller would then tell the warning to the adjacent Centres to which they were connected, where the warnings would be displayed on the display panel by means of coloured lights. This would serve both as an indication that a raid might be approaching before it was plotted on the vertical table, and as a guide to the Warning Officer as to the action which he might have to take on it.

In the event of the total break-down of a R.O.C. Centre, Warning Officers were to proceed to the Emergency Centre to continue operation of the alarm schemes. The Warning Officer at a prescribed adjacent Centre would take over the responsibility for the public warning system for the districts normally covered from the Centre which was out of action. The Royal Observer Corps Liaison Officer at the Fighter Group was responsible for notifying Warning Officers at all Centres adjoining the one which was out of commission of what had occurred. The Warning Officer at the "prescribed" Centre then became immediately responsible for covering the districts concerned.

This system remained in force until the official closing down both of the National Air Raid Warning System and of the Industrial Alarm Scheme on May 2nd 1945.

Re-organisation of the Royal Observer Corps 1942-1942

As the appointment of a new Commandant to the Royal Observer Corps involved major changes to every section of the Corps, it is proposed to deal with the subject in some detail.

The new Commandant of the Royal Observer Corps was confronted with a task of extreme difficulty, and one that required delicacy of handling. He was a serving officer in the Royal Air Force dealing with Civilians, working in an organisation which though efficient, was some way short of maximum efficiency owing to what might fairy be described as the "Club" atmosphere that prevailed. The emphasis that had, in the past, been placed on preserving the Civilian element of the Corps, had brought with it, inevitably, several major disadvantages. It would be unfair to characterize one of these disadvantages as lack of discipline, but it is difficult to define it in any other way. Undoubtedly, certain members of the Corps considered that they had a right as civilians, to write directly, if they thought themselves aggrieved, to the Commandant, or even to Members of Parliament.

It must be remembered that the general level of the performance of the Royal Observer Corps was high, but it must also be realised that it was within the power of part-time members to resign, and it is difficult to see how this could reasonably be tolerated in the third year of a major war. It appeared obvious that a necessary change was the re-organisation of the Corps on a non-military basis, but with graded ranks, and to endeavour thus to instil a somewhat higher standard of esprit-de-corps, and, of even more importance, to attempt by this means to raise the "face-value" of the Royal Observer Corps in the eyes of other regular service formations. There is little doubt that the Corps as a whole had, probably correctly, considered themselves neglected and their work, being unobtrusive, had tended rather to be obscured by the more spectacular work performed by other civilian organisations. A general tightening up of the Headquarters organisation also appeared to be necessary, and a more definite allocation of duties and responsibilities was essential, and, at the same time, it appeared of value to endeavour to bring closer the affiliation between the Royal Observer Corps and the Royal Air Force by making Observer Areas conform more accurately to those of the fighter groups.

Training had, up to this time, been voluntary, and largely organised and run by the Royal Observer Corps Club. This must obviously be the responsibility of Headquarters, Royal Observer Corps, and, equally obviously, must be compulsory, in order that all Observers might conform to the accepted standard of efficiency.

The Commandant submitted a memorandum, on July 6th, 1942, in which he summarized the major problems which, in his opinion, necessitated changes in the policy and organisation of the Corps. In this memorandum he drew up a suggested framework for the re-organization, though he realised that this was likely to be modified as time went on, and as he acquired a more detailed knowledge of the working of the Royal Observer Corps.

It is sufficient, at this stage, to give his conclusions and the summary of the recommendations which were made and which were summarized under eighteen headings. In most cases the reasons behind the recommendations are implicit in the recommendations themselves. He believed that certain changes were necessary in order to increase the efficiency of the Corps beyond its present level. It was possible that some of the recommendations would appear radical and would be therefore best made slowly. With the possibility of technical dislocation of the Radio Location System, the Royal Observer Corps would become more important than before, and it was therefore most necessary that desirable changes should be made quickly.

The present organization of the Royal Observer Corps, as far as the part-time members were concerned, was based on personality and goodwill. Changes of policy might easily upset this and result in wholesale resignations. Though he had the highest regard for the voluntary system in peace-time, the Commandant had doubts as to its certainty under the present, and possible future, conditions of war.

Summary of Recommendations
(i)   Re-organization of R.O.C. Headquarters.

(ii)   Provision of a R.A.F. Serving Officer as Deputy Commandant.

(iii)   Provision of Assistant to Deputy Commandant.

(iv)   Re-organization of Area Headquarters.

(v)   Area Territory to conform with the appropriate Fighter Group territory.

(vi)   Area Headquarters to be housed at appropriate Fighter Groups.

(vii)   Group Headquarters to be housed at Centres.

(viii)   Reservation of Post personnel to be on an individual basis.

(ix)   Employment of mobile young women at Centres.

(x)   Duty Controllers and Table Supervisors to be regarded as Key Men, and reserved irrespective of age.

(xi)   Training to become compulsory and the official liability of the Headquarters Royal Observer Corps as well as the interest of the R.O.C. Clubs.

(xii)   Training pay to be admissible to part-time (B) members.

(xiii)   Training organization.

(xiv)   Provision of efficiency badges.

(xv)   Re-Organisation of the Royal Observer Corps on a non-military basis, but with graded ranks.
(xvi)   R.O.C. Employment Order 1941 to be amended to cover part-time (B) members.
(xvii) Provision of Conditions of Service Regulations.
(xviiii) Message by C.A.S. (This to allay an impression amongst the members that the function of the Corps was diminishing in importance in view of the development of Radio Location, and to stress the necessity for a high standard of individual training from each member of the Royal Observer Corps).

Adjustment of Area Territory
The first of these recommendations to be put into effect was an adjustment of Area Territory to establish closer conformity between Fighter Groups and R.O.C. Areas. This measure was also taken in view of the proposed Inland Reporting Scheme, and the subsequent partial abandonment of that scheme did not detract from the improvement in the correlation of information derived from the adjustments of territory. The changes made were as follows:

(a) Scottish Area   to lose No.36 Group, (Dunfermline)
                                No.34 Group, (Glasgow)
                                No.31 Group, (Galashiels)
(b) Northern Area   to lose No.32 Group, (Carlisle)
                                No.29 Group, (Lancaster)
                                No.8 Group, (Leeds)
                                No.10 Group, (York)
                       to gain No.36 Group, (Dunfermline)
                                No.34 Group, (Glasgow)
                                No.31 Group, (Galashiels)
(c) North Western Area lose Nil
                       to gain No.32 Group, (Carlisle)
                                No.29, Group (Lancaster)
(d) Midland Area   to lose Nil
                       to gain No.8 Group, (Leeds)
                                No.10 Group, (York)

No changes were to be made in the Western and Southern areas, which corresponded roughly with the areas of Nos. 10 and 11 Fighter Groups respectively.

Moves of R.O.C. Headquarters
The next logical alteration was the move of R.O.C. Headquarters to locations in close proximity to Fighter Group Headquarters, and this involved the following moves:

(a) Scottish Area Headquarters from Edinburgh to No.14 (F) Group, R.A.F., Inverness.
(b) Northern Area Headquarters from Catterick to No.13 (F) Group, R.A.F., Newcastle.
(c) Midland Area Headquarters from Grantham to No.12 (F) Group, R.A.F., Watnall.
(d) Western Area Headquarters from Gloucester to No.10 (F) Group, R.A.F., Rudloe.

No changes were necessary in the cases of Southern Area Headquarters and North-Western Area Headquarters whose location at Uxbridge and Preston respectively corresponded with the Headquarters of Nos. 11 and 9 Fighter Groups of the Royal Air Force.

Closing Down of Northern Area R.O.C.
Although this did not take place until July 1st 1943, it should here be mentioned that on that date, No. 13 Fighter Group, R.A.F., ceased to function, and consequently the Northern Area of the Royal Observer Corps was abolished, its groups being re-allocated as follows:

Scottish Area	gained Nos.	36 (Dunfermline)
		34 (Glasgow)
		31 (Galashiels)
		33 (Ayr)
Midland Area	gained Nos.	30 (Durham) and
		9 (York)

With the exception, of course, of the closing down of the Northern

Area, all the other changes specified above took place before the end of 1942.

Memoranda Nos. 1, 2, and 3
As the result of a great deal of investigation and discussion based on his submissions in July 1942, the Commandant submitted to the Air Officer Commanding-in-Chief, on October 20th 1942, for his consideration, three memoranda under the following headings:

Re-organisation of the Royal Observer Corps Area Headquarters – Memorandum No.1
Re-organisation of the Royal Observer Corps Group Headquarters – Memorandum No.2
Training of Royal Observer Corps Post Personnel – Memorandum No.3

The three subjects covered by the memoranda was part of the same scheme and inherently dependent on each other, and he considered that the implementing of the proposals contained therein was absolutely necessary, and, in his opinion, all changes in policy in the Royal Observer Corps should be completed by the end of the current year. It would then be possible to devote the time thereafter to building up on the basis of the changed conditions:

(i)   *Memorandum No.1.* Dealing with the re-organization of Area Headquarters, the Commandant recommended that, in place of the present establishment of an Area Commandant and two Deputy Commandants dividing between them geographically the Observer Groups for which they were responsible, there should be an Area Commandant and one Deputy Commandant, the latter to be charged with Operations and Training. He considered that, in addition, the Deputy Commandant should, from time to time, assist the Royal Observer Corps Liaison Officers in their duties. The R.O.C. L.O's should, in his opinion be reduced from five to four in number. He recommended the establishment of two additional

103

officers, an Operations Staff Officer, who would be responsible for the training of R.O.C. Post and Centre personnel, and an Adjutant. The Administrative Staff, consisting of an Equipment Officer and an Administrative Officer should remain as at present.

(ii) *Memorandum No.2.* The section of recommendations dealing with the re-organization of R.O.C. Groups is probably the most important. Up to that time a system of dual control was in force, by which the Centre Controller was responsible for the Operations Room, while the Observer Group Officer was responsible for the Posts which supplied information to the Operations Room. As both these officers were equal in command and status, any controversial matters, which often owed their origin to that division within the Group, had to be referred to the Area Deputy Commandant.

It was recommended, therefore, that a Group Commandant should be appointed, who would be assisted by an Adjutant. The post of Controller was to be retained, and the Controller would act as Deputy Commandant, while the post of Deputy Controller would be abolished. Further the rank of Duty Controller should be upgraded to that of Officer in view of his heavy operational responsibilities.

The existing post of Observer Group Officer should be abolished, and the number of Assistant O.G.Os should be increased to a maximum of one for every ten posts, and these officers were to be directly responsible to the Group Commandant for the operational efficiency of their sections of Posts.

It was only intended to implement the proposals (if authority was given for this) as and when the changes were deemed to be expedient. Some Groups were ready for an immediate change, while in others the finding of suitable personnel was likely to take time.

(iii) *Memorandum No.3.* There existed at that time no organized system of training Post Personnel, and the intention expressed in this Memorandum was to institute and carry out a comprehensive system of training to include instruction in: (a) Post Procedure; (b) Standing Orders and Current Instruction; (c) Aircraft Recognition.

In addition, a minimum standard of efficiency in Post Procedure and in Aircraft Recognition was to be established, a standard which, with certain reservations, every Post Observer would be expected to reach and maintain. The Officers responsible for the implementing of this recommendation had already been detailed in Memorandum Nos. 1 and 2, and they were the Operations Staff Officers at Area Headquarters and the A.O.G.O's at Groups. In addition, an officer at R.O.C. Headquarters was responsible for the organization of training Post Personnel throughout the Royal Observer Corps.

The duties of A.O.G.O's were given in detail and, amongst others, they included the responsibility for the appointment of Post Instructors and for their efficiency. The latter were responsible to their A.O.G.O for the training of their Post. They were to be known as Leading Observers (when not the Post Head Observer) and were to wear two stripes on the uniform to denote their rank.

The other recommendations made by the Commandant in this Memorandum may be summarized as follows:

(i) Compulsory Instructors' Courses for A.O.G.O's and a definite age limit of 50 for all future appointments.
(ii) Post Meetings to be held once weekly.
(iii) Three separate tests to be instituted for R.O.C. Post Personnel, to be known as Basic, Intermediate, and Master Tests.
(iv) Post Personnel to pay periodical visits to their Centres.
(v) Inter-post visits and competitions to be instituted.
(vi) Proficiency badges to be awarded to those Observers passing the Master Test in Aircraft Recognition.

Approval by the Air Council
After correspondence and discussions had taken place on these three memoranda, and various modifications had been made, general approval was given for the re-organisation of the Royal Observer Corps as outlined, on January 31st 1943.

The Increased Commitments of the Royal Observer Corps

At the end of his first six months' duty as Commandant of the Royal Observer Corps, Air Commodore Ambler rendered a report to Headquarters, Fighter Command, in which he made recommendations regarding the increased commitments of the Corps.

He commenced by giving a brief outline of the duties of the R.O.C. at the beginning of the war which were as follows:

(i) *Posts* – To report the position of aircraft continuously to the Centres and co-operate in this duty with those Posts on the same telephone circuit. Aircraft recognition as understood in 1942 was not the official duty of the Observers on Posts.

(ii) *Centres* – To "Tell" required tracks of friendly aircraft and all hostile and unidentified aircraft, simultaneously to a Fighter Group and Sector Operations Room. The reporting of crashes and other unusual incidents were also the responsibility of the Centre.

There had been no increases in the communications necessary for those tasks since the outbreak of the war.

A list of the duties that had been subsequently added to Posts and Centres were as follows:

POSTS
(i) Aircraft Recognition.
(ii) Liaison with Coastguards.
(ii) Satellite Posts.
(iv) Air Raid Alarm to factories.
(v Air Raid Warnings (31 posts on the South Coast).
(vi) Rockets for low-flying enemy aircraft (69 Posts)
(vii) 'Darky', sets for communicating with aircraft lost or in distress. (29 Posts scheduled, 16 fitted).
(viii)Homing searchlights (107 Posts).
(ix) Reports on aircraft in distress.
(x) G.L. Sets (10 Posts).
(xi) Passing of Army messages in anti-invasion operations.

(xii) Warnings to Home Guard.

(xiii) Warnings to Bomber Command, and others, by direct lines, to posts by local arrangements.

CENTRES

(i)   Reports of bombs and flares.

(ii)   Reports to Groups of air raid warnings originated by posts.

(iii) Liaison between Alarm Controller at the Centre, and Posts.

(iv) G.L. interrogation.

(v)   Air Raid Warnings to Bomber Groups etc.

(vi) Liaison with Gun Operations Rooms.

(vii) Liaison about aircraft in distress with Bomber Groups and Stations; and with regional Commissioners, Police, etc.

In addition to all this Posts had, at fixed times, to give to Centres, and Centres to pass on to Fighter Groups fairly detailed meteorological reports.

The Commandant rightly stated that this great increase in the original commitments, with no corresponding increase in facilities, was slowing down the work of the R.O.C. and jeopardizing the success of its primary function, which was the reporting of enemy aircraft to Fighter Command.

These views were forwarded by the Air Officer Commanding-in-Chief, Fighter Command, to the Air Ministry, the former stating that he was in full agreement with the recommendations which the Commandant made in the latter part of his report, and asking that an early ruling might be given. The recommendations which the A.O.C.-in-C., detailed were as follows:

(1)   The policy of adding satellite posts to existing R.O.C. Posts was not producing the results anticipated and, except in the case of selected Coastguard Posts, should be reversed. An investigation was being instituted into the need for re-siting some of the existing R.O.C. Posts.

(2)   A.A. Command had been told of the need to eliminate all liaison lines between G.O.R.s or gun sites and R.O.C.

Centres or Posts, and to provide only to G.O.R.s, which required R.O.C. information vitally at first hand, a telling line from R.O.C. Centres.

(3) The principle that R.O.C. centres should tell raid information to all recipients on a common multiphone broadcast had been approved, and a request for the necessary G.P.O. apparatus would be submitted.

(4) The problem of providing Bomber Command Groups with raid information to enable them to counter enemy intruder operations was under consideration.

(5) Despite the recurring requests from other Commands or from Civil Authorities for raid information to be passed to them from Centres or Posts, it was considered essential that the following principles should be laid down:

(i) Telephone Communication from each R.O.C. Post (i) should be strictly limited to one R.O.C. Centre and, in a few selected cases, to one Coastguard Station.

(ii) Local Air Raid Warnings, when given by R.O.C. Posts, should be effected by pressing a button, and never by passing a telephone message.

(iii) When Air Raid Warnings are given by the R.O.C. the reports to be made by R.O.C. personnel should be limited to a minimum, and the present requirements should be reviewed and reduced.

(iv) No liaison lines from R.O.C. Centres should be permitted except to selected Fighter Groups and Sectors.

(v) When a request was made for the passing of R.O.C. information to recipients other than to Fighter Command, Groups or Sectors, such a facility should not be granted except in essential cases, and then by means of linking the new "subscriber" to the multiphone broadcast at the appropriate R.O.C. Centre.

(vi) All lines to R.O.C. Centres and Posts not conforming to the abovementioned principles should be recovered. It was estimated that this would involve the recovery of some 200 lines of varying lengths.

(vii) The A.O.C.-in-C., considered that no additional commitments should be undertaken by the R.O.C. except upon his specific recommendation.

These recommendations were approved in principle with the proviso that repercussions were to be avoided in altering speech lines to factories to bell circuits. Where unofficial speech warning lines existed to factories, it was stressed that the Commandant, R.O.C., or his representative, must in each case explain the reason for the change to the factory management concerned, and that no alteration should be made until any serious objection by the management had been removed.

Introduction of Rank Gradings and New Badges of Rank for Officers and Observers

It was decided to introduce rank gradings for officers and observers, with new badges of rank, and to make the wearing of uniform, by officers on duty, compulsory, with effect from March 4th 1943.

Re-organization of the Royal Observer Corps – Promulgation

The recommendations of the Commandant regarding the changes in the organisation of the Corps were promulgated in an Air Ministry Order on March 4th, 1943, and the various appointments, with the appropriate rank of the appointments, were detailed in paragraph 5 of that A.M.O.

Memoranda No. 4 and 5

Two further memoranda dealing with re-organization were submitted to the Air Officer Commanding-in-Chief, Fighter Command, and forwarded by him to the Under Secretary of State for Air on May 14th 1943. These memoranda came under the following headings:-

Re-organisation of Royal Observer Corps Centre crews – Memorandum No.4.

Training of Royal Observer Corps Centre Observers and crews – Memorandum No.5.

It was considered by the A.O.C.-in-C., that the proposals made would, if implemented, greatly improve the organization and efficiency of Centre Operations Rooms.

Memorandum No.4.
The vast increase, since the outbreak of war, in the operational responsibilities thrust upon the Duty Controller made it necessary to bring into effect a devolution of these responsibilities to those Observers working under him. While this devolution had, to some extent, taken place it was considered essential to define more clearly the duties and responsibilities of the Key Observers in R.O.C. Centres, and thus prevent overlapping and confusion. Coincident with this, it was proposed to give appropriate ranks in keeping with the responsibilities of each individual.

The Duty Controller	This Observer, already upgraded to the rank of Observer Officer (in the case of the Centre Controller, Observer Lieutenant) had the following duties:
	(a) He would be responsible for the efficiency of the Centre crew and the efficient working of the whole Group controlled from that Centre during his tour of duty, including the efficient working of all the Posts feeding that Centre.
	(b) While on duty he represented the Group Commandant.
	(c) He would be responsible for working with the R.O.C.L.O. on duty at the Fighter Group.
	(d) His duties fell into two classes, firstly for the input of information into the R.O.C. Centre and, secondly, for the output of information to Fighter Group, Sectors, and other R.A.F. authorities, and it was proposed that he should hold one

	Observer responsible for each of those two functions.
Post Controller	He would be responsible for the input of information from Posts to the Centre and for the taking over of tracks from other Centres. By the use of a key board he would be able, at any time, to listen in to any Post Circuit and to speak to any Post Observer or Plotter. He should hold the rank of Chief Observer.
Assistant Duty Controller	This Observer would be held responsible for the output of information from the Centre, for the efficient working of the Tellers, and for liaison with the R.O.C. Liaison Tellers situated in the Sector Operations Rooms. In the absence of the Duty Controller he would assume the responsibilities of that officer. He should hold the rank of Chief Observer.

R.O.C. Liaison Tellers in the Fighter Sectors
Both the name and the duties of these Observers would remain unchanged under the new proposals, but it was proposed that they should be upgraded to the rank of Chief Observer, in view of the responsibility of their position.

Floor Supervision
The duties of this Observer comprised the supervision of the discipline of all persons employed on the lower floor of the Centre Operations Room, and of the arrangements for the provision of raid plaques, counters, and so on, to Plotters' requirements. He would work directly under the Duty Controller and would also take instructions from the Post Controller.

Memorandum No.5
The training of Post Personnel has been dealt with under Memorandum No.3, and in this Memorandum the

Commandant dealt with the subject of training as it affected Centre Observer and crews. No system existed for their training at that time, and, in most cases, it had been the joint responsibility of Centre Controllers and Duty Controllers. It was considered that the selection and training should be no less exacting than that obtaining for R.A.F. and W.A.A.F. Plotters in R.A.F. Filter Rooms.

It was felt that a satisfactory standard could be attained if a woman instructor were appointed at each R.O.C. Centre who, before her appointment, had attended and qualified at the Leighton Buzzard Training School, and would thenceforward be able to give instruction on R.A.F. lines.

It was, at the same time, considered essential to organise a scheme for giving progressive instruction to existing members and to make provision for such specialised instruction as it might be found necessary to introduce from time to time.

The comprehensive scheme submitted was divided into three parts:

(i) Preliminary training of recruits.
(ii) Specialised instruction for (a) Duty Controllers and (b) Centre Instructors (women)
(iii) Normal progressive instruction for Centre Observers and Crews designed to follow a line parallel to that being undertaken for Post members.

The Duty Controller would be required to take such tests as might, from time to time, be laid down by R.O.C. Headquarters, and to attend such courses of instruction as might be required by their Group Commandants. They would be responsible to the Centre Controller for the normal training of their Crews.

The Centre Instructors (women) would select and give preliminary instruction to recruits and give special instruction on the subjects taught at the W.A.A.F. Course to any members sent to them for that purpose by the Centre Controller. They would also exercise general supervision of the welfare of the women observers at the Centre.

The scope of the proposals was limited to the provision of a Basic Test, though an Intermediate and Master Test, parallel with those obtaining in the Post Training Scheme, were envisaged for the future.

The Basic Test would be divided into six parts:

(i)   Ability to plot or tell at a rate of 10 plots per minute without ancillary information (e.g. plan position but no height, strength etc.)
(ii)   Ability to fill at least two different positions in the Centre.
(iii) Possession of a fair knowledge of Centre procedure.
(iv)   Possession of an elementary knowledge of the History of the R.O.C.
(v)   Possession of an elementary knowledge of either (a) Post Procedure or (b) The working of a Sector Operations Room.
(vi)   Possession of an elementary knowledge of, and the ability to recognise from silhouettes and photographs, 20 types of aircraft correctly from an episcope showing of 30 selected from those contained in the list for the Posts' Basic Test.

Approval by the Air Council
The proposals contained in Memoranda Nos. 4 and 5 were approved by the Air Council, on August 28th 1943, with the omission of the proposal concerning the appointment of Centre Instructor (woman), as it was not considered that this establishment was necessary at that time.

Group Officers (Women)
It became necessary very shortly to press for the appointment of what were to be called eventually Women Personnel Officers and this point was raised again with success in September 1943.

At that time, as it was pointed out, there were over 2,000 women in the Royal Observer Corps, of whom approximately 90% were employed at Centres. In view of the fact that their pay and conditions of service did not compare favourably with those obtaining for industry, it was all the more important to exercise care for their welfare, and extreme tact and consideration was therefore necessary in their management. The duties of these officers were to include:

(i)   Responsibility to the Group Commandant for all matters connected with women personnel and, in addition for all preliminary training of recruits.

(ii)   Any special training of existing members at the request of the Group Commandant.

(iii)   Responsibility for all billeting arrangements for all mobile women at Centres.

(iv)   Acting in an advisory capacity to the Group Officer (Formerly known as A.O.G.O) on his visits to Posts at which women were serving.

(v)   Conducting, or being present at, all interviews of women candidates.

(vi)   Keeping in close touch with the local Ministry of Labour and National Service Manageress.

Change of Commandant, Royal Observer Corps
During the course of the re-organization which was being effected in the Royal Observer Corps, Air Commodore Ambler was succeeded in his position of Commandant by Air Commodore Finlay Crerar, C.B.E., who was to occupy this position from June 24th 1943 until November 8th 1945, thus carrying on the new system of having a serving officer in the Royal Air Force as Commandant of this civilian Corps.

Track Designations
With the increasing air traffic it became necessary to revise the system of track designations which had been operative, with occasional modifications, since the outbreak of war. By this new system each track was designated with a Serial Number which it retained irrespective of change of identity. Its identity was indicated by a prefix letter, thus allowing for rapid changes of track identity without interfering with track number continuity.

Immediately a track was picked up by the Air Reporting Organization a serial number was allotted to it, without regard to the identity of the aircraft. The identity was then indicated by the addition of a prefix letter, the number remaining unchanged, whenever practicable, except in the case of friendly aircraft with a R.O.C. designation which crossed into the Radar area. Each Group Filter Room and each R.O.C. Centre was to hold a block of

Serial Numbers, to be allotted in turn to tracks established by it. Serial Numbers held by R.O.C. Centres consisted of the numerals from 10 to 99 inclusive followed by a Centre letter indicating the name of the Centre.

In R.O.C. Centres Serial Numbers were to be allotted by the plotter and the track would then retain that serial number, complete with the suffix letter denoting the Centre of origin, notwithstanding that it passed into another R.O.C. Centre area.

Identification letters were to be allotted by the Duty Controller only, under the following conditions:

Hostile (a) Aircraft clearly observed to be of hostile type.
(b) Aircraft clearly observed to bear the markings of an enemy air force.
(c) Aircraft observed to commit a hostile act.

Friendly (a) Aircraft clearly observed to be of friendly type.
(b) Aircraft clearly observed to bear the markings of British or Allied Aircraft.
(c) Aircraft identified as friendly, by radio signal (i.e. I.F.F.).
(d) Aircraft identified as friendly by behaviour, i.e. previous recognition coupled with continuous tracking by R.O.C. Centres.

Aircraft not recognised as positively hostile or friendly were to be told by the R.O.C. Centres by the Serial Number (prefixed with the word "Serial") until an Identification Letter was allotted by the Fighter Group concerned. In cases where a track split, one track was to continue with the Allotted Serial Number, while the other portion received the next Serial Number available at the Filter Room or R.O.C. Centre in whose area the split occurred. The same Identification Letter would be retained as on the original track until rectified as necessary.

It tracks with the same Identification Letter combined into one formation the resulting track was to be continued with the Serial Number of the track with the greatest number of aircraft. If, on the other hand, tracks with different Identification Letters combined, the track was to be continued with the Identification Letter and Serial Number of the operationally more important track.

Should hostile and friendly fighter tracks merge, the resultant track was to be told with the original hostile track serial and the Identification Letter 'M' (for 'Mix-up').

Rules were also laid down for the colouring of letters and of plaques for track display, for allocation of Track Serial Numbers and Centre Letters and for Teleprinter Procedure.

Thus the whole system of Track Designations was put on a comprehensive basis, and this system, with modifications when experience proved them necessary, was continued for the remainder of the war.

Safety of Aircraft

With the growing strength of the bomber offensive and with the arrival of the United States [Army] Air Force, the Royal Observer Corps was put to its greatest test, not only through the enormous increase in flying generally, but also through the vigilance and accuracy of plotting necessary to bring home safely damaged or lost aircraft.

Many were the occasions on which badly damaged bombers, with crews wounded, returning from raids over enemy territory, were landed safely owing to the work of the Observer Posts and Centres.

Probably the principal value of the Corps lay in the ability of trained Observers to distinguish by sound aircraft with faulty engines, or aircraft flying erratically, and the accurate information as to position, course, and height of such aircraft was the main factor that enabled other more scientific methods to be brought into action for the purpose of homing. The sentence so frequently used: "The engine sounds wrong" was no mere formula, in the majority of cases the information was accurate.

In the early days of the war the use to which the Corps was put, as far as aircraft safety was concerned, was very limited. This was due to the lack of organized safety methods and unified control. Early in 1941 a Flying Control Liaison Section was established at Fighter Groups, and the officers of these sections worked in the closest touch with the Royal Observer Corps Liaison Officers in the Fighter Group Operations Rooms. The Flying Control Liaison Officer was made the sole authority for initiating distress action, because of his specialized knowledge of aircraft safety procedure, and of airfields and their equipment. He was able to use the information provided by the Royal Observer Corps to the best advantage, thus minimizing the risk of duplication and consequent confusion to pilots.

Every measure possible was also taken to keep the Royal Observer Corps informed of the facilities available to assist aircraft, and arrangements were made for Observers to visit airfields and Groups, while lectures and talks were given to members of the Corps all over the country by Flying Control Liaison Officers, one such officer alone addressing over 20,000 members from 1941 until the end of the war.

There were three main aids supplied to the Royal Observer Corps in order to help them with the actual work of homing aircraft. Certain Posts in the North-East were equipped with searchlights for indicating direction to aircraft in distress; this was in the Midland Area of the Corps, as area which contained a large proportion of the bomber aerodromes.

In 1943 about fifty Posts were supplied with T.R.G. R/T Sets, known as "Darky" sets. These Posts were chosen on account of their geographical position in districts where the normal "Darky" cover was sparse. A listening watch was kept during the hours of darkness and, at some Posts, by day also. On receipt of a call for assistance the aircraft would be given its position and a course to steer to the nearest airfield fit for landing. These sets were used on many occasions and proved of great value.

Later in 1943, a system of ground flares operated by R.O.C. Observers was instituted at about 340 Posts in hilly or mountainous districts. This use of red flares was known by the code name of "Granite", and the Posts were instructed to fire the flares when aircraft were thought to be in danger of flying into high ground, or approaching high ground at an unsafe height. Although the actual operation of the flares was carried out by the Post Observers, sometimes on their own initiative, the success of the scheme was, of course, dependent on the careful observation and continuity of tracking performed by the Centre.

Chapter 9

January 1944 to May 1945

In this chapter it is proposed to deal with enemy activity over this country up to the date of the invasion of Europe and the beginning of the flying bomb attack.

After the three months' lull there was a recrudescence of hostile activity and the January total of enemy sorties (611) was higher than that of any month in the previous year. Of this total probably some 340 aircraft operated over land and two-thirds of this effort was directed against London in two large scale attacks on the nights of January 21st/22nd and 29th/30th.

Again, in February, the German effort was more than doubled and London was the main target on the seven nights of large scale effort, on each of which more than 130 aircraft penetrated over land. The proportion of enemy aircraft destroyed was over 5% in both these months, as it was also in March, though now the number of sorties began to drop and London was only the main target on four nights. South-West England and South Wales, with a small concentration over Bristol, were the main targets on one night of this month.

In April, once more, the effort diminished, to 888 sorties, and this month the enemy directed his activities to Plymouth and the invasion ports while, despite the fact that penetration over land was not deep, his casualties still totalled over 5% of his effort. During the next month London was clear of bombing, and there was small scale intruder activity in East Anglia, while minelaying and large scale shipping reconnaissances were carried out by enemy aircraft.

In the invasion month, June, the total of enemy sorties had dropped to 271, of which some 220 were devoted to reconnaissance. So much for the hostile activity by night against the United Kingdom, while by day, apart from the naval shipping and weather reconnaissances which increased in scale towards the month of June, enemy activity was negligible.

Improved Raid Reporting Organization

It had been decided on January 29th 1943 to centralize all identification by moving the Royal Observer Corps Liaison Officer from each Group Operations' Room to the appropriate Filter Room. By the provision of an inland table in the Filter Room, with information obtained by 'teeing-off' from the plotting circuits from Observer Centres to Group Operations Room, the R.O.C. L.O. and the Filter Room Controller would then be of mutual assistance in identifying aircraft.

It was, however, considered inadvisable, as regards No. 11 Fighter Group, to implement this scheme fully, as any initial difficulties in operation would arise just when operational activity was at its height, with the prospect of an invasion of Europe in the near future. Accordingly, though it was proposed to continue with the provision of an inland table and the necessary communications, it was decided to postpone the move of the R.O.C. L.O. to the Filter Room to a more convenient occasion.

No. 11 Fighter Group was rather peculiarly placed in this respect, as its Filter Room was at Stanmore while its Operations Room was at Uxbridge, whereas in the other Fighter Groups both Departments were in the same building.

Telling and Display of Individual Tracks and Area Raids

In the month of January, two Operational Procedure Instruction No. 1 and 2 of 1944 were produced, by Headquarters, Air Defence of Great Britain, dealing with the "Telling and Display of Individual Tracks" and "Area Reporting" respectively. In that vital time it was essential to bring up to date and standardize all methods of display in order that the whole system should work harmoniously when the actual invasion operation commenced.

The object envisaged in issuing the Instructions was to introduce improved and extended methods of area reporting in view of the ever increasing volume of air information to be dealt with over both land and sea.

It is not proposed to discuss the details of these instructions, as they consisted largely in bringing up to date all existing instructions, on the subjects, and provided, in fact, one standard modified text on each of the subjects to replace the many existing instructions dealing with separate aspects. It may, however, be of interest to summarize the 'Intention' as laid down in Instructions Nos. 1 and 2:

> *A.D.G.B. Operational Procedure Instruction No. 1/1944*
> To detail the procedure whereby air information reported in the form of individual tracks is to be: (i) Displayed in Filter Rooms and Operations Rooms, and (ii) Told from Filter Rooms, R.O.C. Centres, and Operations Rooms.

> *A.D.G.B. Operational Procedure Instruction No. 2/1944*
> (i) To extend the use of area reporting to inland areas, and to define the conditions under which area reporting may be adopted by Filter Rooms and R.O.C. Centre. (ii) To introduce a method of display which can be used for all areas whether told by Filter Rooms or R.O.C. Centres, and which can be rapidly adopted. (iii) To introduce a system of area raid designations which will indicate the composition of the area.

A distinction was made in A.D.G.B. O.P.1 No. 1/1944 (for the benefit of those Fighter Groups in which the R.O.C. L.O. had been transferred to the Filter Room, and in which the inland table was in operation in the Filter Room) between two types of tracks. This was necessary as the telling from the R.O.C. Centres was received by both the plotters in the Operations Rooms and in the Filter Room. All telling sequences which were to be acted upon in Fighter Group and Sector Operations Rooms were to be prefixed by the word "Operational". Telling sequences spoken for the use of Filter Rooms only were not to be so prefixed.

A.D.G.B. O.P.1 No. 2/1944 dealt with Area Reporting in detail, comprising Mass and Zone Raids, with their display, and with the telling of individual tracks within Area Raids.

Responsibility for Identification of Overland Tracks

In response to a request from No. 12 Fighter Group, a decision was taken, on February 20th 1944, by Headquarters, Air Defence of Great Britain on the question of where the ultimate responsibility should lie for the identification of over land tracks when the R.O.C. L.O. was situated in the Group Filter Room.

It was decided that the final responsibility for overland identification must rest with the Filter Room Controller. It was not, however, intended that the latter should personally identify all overland tracks, but that the R.O.C. L.O. should continue to exercise his normal functions in that respect, only referring to the Filter Room Controller in place of the Group Controller (which had been the previous custom). To ensure smooth working of that system, the Filter Room Controller must keep the R.O.C. L.O. fully informed of all information that might affect the identification of overland tracks, and similarly the R.O.C. L.O. must give the Filter Room Controller all available R.O.C. information upon tracks of doubtful identity.

In practice, it was considered that delegation of authority to the R.O.C. L.O. would tend to be on a fairly permanent basis.

Detection and Reporting of Pilotless Aircraft

In May 1944, an Operational Procedure Instruction was issued dealing with the Detection and Reporting of Pilotless Aircraft. For the procedure to be adopted in the event of the enemy using this form of attack the code word "Diver" was used and the subject is dealt with later in this narrative.

Liaison between G.C.I. Stations and R.O.C. Centres

As a result of an investigation carried out by the Operational Research Section of Fighter Command, details of which were contained in their Report No. 24 and Addendum thereto, it was decided to establish liaison circuits between some 20 G.C.I. Stations and 28 R.O.C. Centres. It was considered that this would improve the efficiency of the Raid Reporting Organization and, speaking generally, the scheme was designed to fill in the gaps in either source of information.

At each G.C.I. Station an operator known as the "R.O.C. Agent" was required to pass to his associated R.O.C. Centre or Centres such information regarding the plan position, height and identification of aircraft flying within range of his station as either:

(i)   He might consider to be of value to the Centre, or
(ii) The Centre might request him to supply.

Similarly he was to obtain from "G.C.I. Liaison" at the appropriate R.O.C. Centre such information as the Controller at his G.C.I. Station might require, and also arrange for running commentaries to be given by such R.O.C. Centre (in the same manner as was customary in the case of running commentaries given to Sectors) in accordance with his Controller's instructions.

The Flying Bomb.
As has been previously mentioned, provision was made, in an Operational Procedure Instruction issued on May 18th 1944, for the possibility that the enemy might attack this country with pilotless aircraft. The probable launching sites were believed to extend from Dunkerque down to Dieppe, and from the Cherbourg peninsula area. It was believed that the likely targets would be London and the Bristol area.

It was also expected that, as pilotless aircraft could operate in conditions which would exclude operations by normal aircraft, the enemy might take advantage of such conditions. Extreme vigilance was therefore required even during periods when our own aircraft were grounded.

To assist in the procedure being instituted to cope with this threat, an inland table (similar to that already in operation in No.10 (F) Group Filter Room) was to be installed in No.11 (F) Group Filter Room so that immediate information from R.O.C. sources (as well as Radar) concerning pilotless aircraft could be centralized in whichever of these two Filter Rooms was appropriate.

Also direct circuits were being installed between the No.11 Group Filter Room, and Biggin Hill Sector Operations Room and between the No.10 Group Filter Room and Middle Wallop Sector Operations Room. The Operational Procedure Instruction then proceeded to detail the action to be taken by each part of the reporting System, using the code name "Diver" and ensuring that the information that "Diver" procedure was in force was known to all concerned with the minimum of delay. Once again it was considered that Running Commentaries from R.O.C. Centres would be of value, and should be given to Sector Controllers to assist in the interception of pilotless aircraft over land.

Instructions were also given for the type of display to be used on Operations Rooms Tables to distinguish the tracks of pilotless aircraft from other tracks and, in an appendix, a description was given of the probable appearance, speed (both maximum and average), operational height, and flying path of such aircraft. As the story of the "Diver" attack on this country has been told elsewhere, it is proposed to confine this description to the part played by the Royal Observer Corps in the operations.

Flying Bomb Activities June 15th to 22nd, 1944.
An analysis of the first week of the attack was made by the Operational Research Section (A.D.G.B.) and from this analysis several points of interest emerged.

The first flying bombs, fired from the Pas de Calais in the early hours of June 13th fell on Southern England, and there was no further activity from that time until just after sunset on June 15th. It may be mentioned here that the first flying bomb was picked up and reported by the Observers on the Dymchurch Observer Post, and the warning given immediately in accordance with the procedure established.

On the night of June 15th, 75 flying bombs exploded on land, and on the following day a further 65. Over the whole week reviewed, the average crash rate was 6 per hour by night and 2½ per hour by day. In those early days there were difficulties in identification, and also a certain amount of disjointed tracking. From the point of view of the Royal Observer Corps there was certainly double tracking in many cases, due to the number of Posts from which any one flying bomb might be visible.

The coastal area over which landfall was usually made was between Dover and Brighton, with the majority between Dymchurch and Beachy Head. As had been anticipated, the flying bombs were, at this time, fired from an area extending from Dunkerque to Rouen. The tracks were very straight over most of the path, with a slight deviation to left or right frequently just before the crash. The average airspeed was shown to be in the neighbourhood of 340 m.p.h.; in practically all cases the airspeed lay between 240 m.p.h. and 400 m.p.h. with rather more over 400 than under 240 m.p.h.

In height there was a remarkable similarity between the height distribution given by Radar at 40 miles from the coast and that given by the Royal Observer Corps at the balloon barrage. It appeared, from each series of estimates, that an appreciable proportion of the bombs flew at 3,000 feet and above, or at 1,000 feet and below.

Royal Observer Corps Tracking.

Identification by the Royal Observer Corps of flying bombs was good and, in fact, no case was found of a bomb coming in without being identified as such, though it was suspected that the "Diver" identification was given frequently to the tracks of friendly aircraft. Most of the tracks were picked up at the coast, and, where tracks appeared to start more than 10 miles inland, these were, in the majority of cases, examples of double tracking. In the matter of hand-over between Radar and the Royal Observer Corps, of the 734 Filter Room tracks considered to be justified as "Diver" tracks 544 were picked up and continued by the Corps.

Commendation by Ministry of Home Security.

In a letter to the Commandant from the Ministry of Home Security appreciation of the tracking was conveyed in the following words: "From the warning point of view I feel it right that I should express how far the admirable tracking of 'Diver' and its displays by the R.O.C. has gone towards making the warning officer's task one which has not been beyond his powers … We have our difficulties, particularly in giving release signals but they are our own difficulties, never ones arising from the display either on horizontal or vertical tables".

Establishment of Control Facilities at R.O.C. Centres.
Amongst many other measures taken to intercept flying bombs, it was decided to establish R.A.F. Controllers at Maidstone and Horsham Observer Centres, the two Centres whose areas covered the majority of the flying bomb activity at that time. The facilities provided consisted of a V.H.F./R.T. twin channel mobile, and a special liaison circuit was provided to Biggin Hill, the R.A.F. Sector principally concerned. Successful trials of control from an Observer Centre had previously been effected at the Lincoln Centre, working in conjunction with Digby R.A.F. Sector of No.12 Fighter Group, and a special protractor designed during those trials was sent to Maidstone for use in interceptions.

A M.E.W. (Microwave Early Warning) Set had, by June 29th, been put into operation at Fairlight, for special analysis purposes in connection with flying bombs, and this was linked with Maidstone and Horsham Observer Centres for checking that the tracks analysed at Fairlight were, in fact, those of flying bombs.

Use of Snowflake Rockets
Snowflake Rockets were used for two purposes by Observer Posts during the anti-Diver operations. Coastal Posts, in certain cases, were already in possession of these rockets, and were now instructed to fire them during the hours of daylight when a pilotless aircraft was sighted within two miles of the post. Thus, as with the tip-and-run raiders, fighter patrols would be warned of the direction of attack.

With the large increase in the balloon barrage to the south-east of London to counter the flying bombs, there was a considerable danger of fighter aircraft, concentrating on interception, flying into the barrage. It was accordingly decided to equip 32 posts on the south, east and west of the 'Diver' Balloon Barrage with Red Snowflake Rockets, to be fired whenever an aircraft within three miles of the post was seen or heard to be approaching in the direction of the barrages. These posts were made up of 17 R.O.C. Posts from the Bromley, Maidstone and Horsham Groups and 15 Wireless Observer Unit Posts.

The precaution was intended primarily for the protection of fighter aircraft in pursuit of flying bombs, but was to be taken in the event of any aircraft being seen to be flying at a height and in

125

a direction which was likely to result in its flying into the barrage.

Lessening of the Vulnerable Area
With the invasion and the capture of the Cherbourg peninsula it was apparent that attacks would no longer be possible from that direction, and it was therefore considered unnecessary for the 'Diver' procedure to remain in force in No. 21 (Exeter) Observer Group.

Elimination of Double Tracking
As has been previously mentioned in this account of Anti-'Diver' Operations, one of the main difficulties with which the Observer Corps had to contend was the tendency towards double tracking. This was particularly prevalent on one of the main avenues of approach, between Pevensey and Fairlight. This "lane" ran almost parallel with the boundary between the Maidstone and Horsham Groups, and it was consequently difficult to avoid over plotting by perimeter posts, with the result that one 'Diver' might easily be tracked by both Centres. Thus confusion was caused to R.A.F. Controllers at Maidstone and Horsham, apart from that experienced by recipients of the 'Telling' broadcast.

It was considered that immediate inter-centre liaison was necessary, and arrangements were therefore made for direct liaison facilities to be provided as follows:

(i)   Maidstone – Horsham
(ii) Maidstone – Bromley
(iii) Horsham – Bromley

With the possibility of the 'Diver' activity moving to the East Coast, as rocket sites were eliminated by the Allied advance on the Continent, it was decided also to provide these direct liaison facilities between Colchester and Bromley Observer Centres.

Withdrawal of R.A.F. Controllers
By September 14th 1944 it became possible to withdraw the R.A.F. Controllers as the flying bomb attack had abated, and the following message was sent from No.11 Fighter Group:- "On the

withdrawal of the R.A.F. Controllers from Maidstone, I should like to say how much the assistance given to them by all the R.O.C. Centre personnel was appreciated. Their co-operation and enthusiasm contributed greatly to the defeat of the flying bombs in that area".

Air-Launched Flying Bombs
With the defeat of the flying bomb attack on the South-East and South of England came the transfer of activity to the East Coast, with the launching of bombs from enemy aircraft flying over the North Sea. Post and Centre personnel of the Midland Area of the Royal Observer Corps were warned of the possibility of these isolated attacks.

Issue of Air Raid Warnings by Certain East Anglian Posts
In certain cases it proved impossible to give proper air raid warnings to coastal districts in East Anglia of the approach of flying bombs launched from aircraft as it proved difficult for Radar to give adequate warning. It was therefore suggested by the Ministry of Home Security that 7 named Coastal Observer Posts should give injected "RED" warnings as for tip-and-run raids during daylight. This proposal was approved on October 14th 1944.

Activity in Midland and North Western Areas
On the night of December 23rd/24th 1944, flying bomb activity was experienced in the Midland and North-Western Areas of the Royal Observer Corps. Though the opinion was held in some quarters that the parent launching aircraft might have penetrated overland, there was no evidence to support this theory. There was certainly no sign of returning tracks. On this occasion flying bombs came over in salvoes, and this resulted in lack of efficiency in hand-over, and initiation of a good many Centre designations.

The flying bombs penetrated over the coast in the Lincoln and York (No. 10) Groups, and went in a general westerly direction, mainly to the Manchester and Liverpool areas. Though it proved difficult, owing to tracking difficulties and 'teething troubles' to decide the total number of tracks, it appeared that there were some 36 crashes in the Midland Area and 32 in the North Western.

The figures for crashes were probably incorrectly filtered, as the Ministry of Home Security could only account for about 30 incidents.

Conclusions

There is no doubt that the flying bomb activity represented a very grave menace to this country, not only because of its destructive powers and its threat to life, but perhaps even more to the incipient danger to the morale of a people who had already experienced five years of war. The part played by the Royal Observer Corps in the defeat of this menace was a very important one, though unspectacular. Firstly, a great deal of hard and intensive work was done by officers and other personnel in explaining and instructing Observers in order that they should be fully proficient in their work when the attack started. Secondly it was vital that the tracking must be accurate and swift as our countermeasures depended largely on information from the Royal Observer Corps, and the Air Raid Warnings and Factory Alerts depended equally on that information. Apart from the actual operation of counter-measures to the flying bomb, it was also important for those in authority to assess the relative merits of individual measures adopted. For this purpose the Corps was used also, to pass not only the plots of crashes, but also whether, in their estimation, the bomb crashed of its own accord, or whether it was destroyed by fighters, anti-aircraft guns, or by the balloon barrage.

The use of Royal Observer Corps Centres as control units for fighters also proved successful as, by their close touch with Observer Posts through the network of communications, Controllers were enabled to give their fighters the most up-to-date information, and their relative position to the flying-bomb.

The use of the Snowflake rockets by Post Observers was also of great value, the white rockets drawing the attention of patrolling fighters to the direction in which the bomb was flying, and the red rockets safeguarding friendly aircraft as they drew near to the balloon barrage. The work of Observers in both Centres and Posts during this period was most arduous, and it is a great tribute to their keenness that a scheme to exchange personnel to ensure periods of rest during this difficult time was withdrawn as those concerned preferred to stay at their work. A small number of volunteers, out of the huge numbers who were anxious to serve, were however, brought in from other Centres unaffected by the flying bombs.

The Rocket Attacks

There is little to say of the work of the Royal Observer Corps during the Rocket Attacks on this country as their work in this connection was confined to recording the crashes and reporting the locality to the correct authorities. It may be of interest to record that on December 29th 1944, six Observer Posts south-east of Manchester, in conditions of extraordinary visibility saw in the air a rocket which exploded in the London area some 200 miles away. It was described by one cluster of posts as 'a white light which appeared to circle and then travel south'.

Chapter 10

R.O.C. Personnel in Seaborne Operations

On April 5th 1944 a meeting was held at the Air Ministry to consider the employment in merchant vessels during operation "Overlord" of Royal Observer Corps personnel, experienced in aircraft recognition.

This proposal had been made originally by the Air Commander-in-Chief, Allied Expeditionary Air Force. His view was that such employment of trained personnel would improve the standard of recognition and, indirectly, ensure better control of anti-aircraft gunfire during the "Overlord" assault. It was estimated that some 2,000 men would be required in all but, while the Admiralty concurred fully in the principle involved in employing trained observers, they considered it unlikely that more than 200 could be accommodated on board. They were, therefore, for their part compelled to limit their requirements to two observers each for such of the 30 L.S.I.(L)'s and some 90 British M.T. Ships in which accommodation was available. The reason for this was that all accommodation on board would be already so overcrowded that even the number of men manning the guns had had to be reduced.

On enquiry it appeared that the United States authorities were also agreeable in principle and that some 300 Observers would be required for United States ships. The question of number was, however, to be taken up further with the United States authorities.

It was agreed that the role of the Observers on board ships would be purely that of advisers on aircraft recognition.

After discussion on the conditions of service to be offered to volunteers for this service it was considered that alternative proposals should be offered for either two months' or one months' initial service, and that they should be employed under a Naval Auxiliary Scheme, details of which should be agreed between the Admiralty and the Air Ministry. Further, it was decided that they should hold the rank of either Petty Officers or Chief Petty Officers, and that instructions to Masters of merchant vessels were to point out that their watchkeeping hours should be so arranged that the maximum of efficiency was obtained from these Observers.

The meeting then discussed in some detail the numerous questions of organization and administration involved in this scheme and the following points were agreed:

(i)   That approval should be requested from the Admiralty for the volunteers to continue to wear their R.O.C. uniform.

(ii) That the Commandant R.O.C. should deal direct with the Admiralty on the details of equipment, such as gas clothing, oilskins, binoculars and so on.

(iii) That the Air Ministry should arrange a control depot where all volunteers should assemble.

(iv) That three R.O.C. officers, at the most, would be required at each Defensively Equipped Merchant Ship (D.E.M.S.) area, i.e. London, Bristol and Southampton.

(v)   That no R.O.C. officer need be stationed at embarkation ports.

(vi) That Observers should be kitted at the central depot.

(vii) That the R.O.C. officers would remain in the Royal Observer Corps.

Among the other points which were considered, and on which decisions were taken, were the questions of pay, casualties and victualling.

Air Ministry Confidential Order A63/1944

Details of the agreed scheme were accordingly promulgated in an A.M.C.O., a copy of which was circulated to all Head Observers, together with a personal message form the Commandant. In the former it was stated that all male members of the Corps, whether whole-time or part-time, and irrespective of rank, were eligible to volunteer, but part-time members would only be accepted if they produced written permission from their employers. All volunteers would be required, before final acceptance, to undergo a medical examination (the standard of which would not be unduly high), and to satisfy the selecting officers as to their proficiency in aircraft recognition.

On receipt of a notice instructing them to do so, volunteers were to proceed to a depot in the south of England (Bournemouth had been chosen). The A.M.C.O. went on to say that the Allied naval and air commanders regarded the scheme as a matter of high operational importance. As a result of the employment of seaborne volunteers, it would be necessary to effect their replacement in order that the operational efficiency of the Royal Observer Corps might remain unimpaired by their absence.

It was stated, therefore, that members who were prevented from volunteering for seaborne service, or whose offer of service could not be accepted, could render valuable assistance by volunteering for temporary transfer to an area from which seaborne volunteers had been released. This was more particularly important in the southern coastal belt. Where the release of seaborne volunteers was particularly heavy, and where it was not possible fully to make good their absence by replacement volunteers, it would be necessary to provide the replacement personnel by compulsory transfer. Powers were being sought to amend the Defence Regulations of 1939 to provide (subject to a right of appeal) that in future any whole-time member of the R.O.C. would be liable to serve in any place in the United Kingdom.

A Personal Message from Commandant R.O.C.

As has been stated above, a personal message from the Commandant, R.O.C., accompanied this A.M.C.O. in which the proposed scheme was put on a less formal basis. As he pointed out, this was a handsome and well-deserved tribute to the skill and value of the Corps to the Fighting Services. It was also the answer to the numerous requests which he had from time to time received to be allowed to take part in more active operations. Inefficient and faulty recognition had contributed largely to enemy successes against our shipping, and also to losses of our own aircraft from friendly fire. He mentioned also that, as had been stated in the A.M.C.O., volunteers would wear R.O.C. uniform with a naval armband and a shoulder flash "Seaborne".

All Head Observers were ordered to bring these details to the notice of all observers immediately, and to impress on them the necessity of volunteering quickly. Supplementary instructions, giving more details of the terms of service, stated that, on enrolment, the Observers were to be known as Aircraft Identifiers, and would be under the Naval Discipline Act, as D.E.M.S. personnel.

In British and European Allied Ships they were to be advisers to the Master on aircraft recognition, while on United States Ships they would fill the same function towards the Armed Guard Officer. They would, in the first instance, be sent to the R.O.C. Depot, Royal Bath Hotel, Bournemouth, where they would be medically examined and enrolled into the Navy. After enrolment they would be kitted up, and given about a week or ten days instruction in general ship matters, seamanship, naval methods of reporting aircraft, security addressing of correspondence when embarked, etc. Their recognition training would also continue.

By May 4th 1944, 475 Observers had volunteered for seaborne duty, and it was anticipated that two batches of 300 selected Observers would report at the depot at Bournemouth on May 8th and May 15th respectively. By May 6th, the number of volunteers had increased to 900, and it was stated that 300 of those had been selected and would report on May 8th.

Volunteers came in steadily and the final figures show that, from the 40 Royal Observer Corps Groups the total number of volunteers was 1094, of whom 81 were rejected on medical grounds, 209 on the trade test, and 8 were withdrawn for various reasons. Or the remaining 796 Aircraft Identifiers, 334 were on one month's engagement and 462 on two months'. Those accepted were posted to 11 different ports, the majority being posted to Southampton, London and Cardiff. Of those rejected 72 volunteered for Coastal Duty and were all posted for that form of service.

In order to facilitate special training of Royal Observer Corps personnel for D.E.M. Ships it was arranged between the Air Ministry and the Admiralty that facilities should be given for the

Commandant, Deputy Commandant and the R.O.C. Officer in charge of the scheme to participate in exercise "Fabius", the preliminary trials for operation "Overlord".

Operation "Overlord"

Accounts of this operation as seen by the Aircraft Identifiers, and looked at from their angle of aircraft recognition, show clearly the vital necessity of the employment on shipping, during operations, of trained observers.

On June 9th 1944 two Aircraft Identifiers aboard a U.S. Ship, the S.S. *John S. Mosby*, M.T. 217 X.U.I. rendered a report to the Commandant, R.O.C. of that evening's happenings off "Utah" Beach, Normandy. They commenced by the hope that some system would be devised that would obviate a recurrence of the unnecessary loss of life and equipment that had taken place. This description may be given verbatim:

> At approximately 20.25 hours we were both on watch on the bridge when the gun look-out reported "two aircraft 45°". We immediately recognised these as Mustangs and reported "P.51 Mustangs". The aircraft were flying West to East along the beach about a mile from the starboard bow.
>
> On drawing nearer they were immediately fired on by small landing craft from the direction of the beach, followed by a devastating fire from practically every other gunner in the area. Markings on the aircraft were clearly visible and the pilot of the nearer aircraft was seen to flash lights from the leading edge of the wings presumably as a warning that he was a friendly aircraft … Both aircraft came in at 500 to 1000 feet, flying in a normal and level manner.
>
> When engaged, they attempted to obtain cover in the clouds, but the fire was so terrific that both were hit, the left hand aircraft crashed into the bay, the pilot bailing out from low level, and being picked up later. The other aircraft, although hit, was lost sight of and its fate unknown'.

Ten minutes later, says the observers' account, there was a repetition of these circumstances, though this time both aircraft crashed, the pilots having no chance of escape.

Between that time and 22.15 hours, approximately, there were four more occasions on which friendly aircraft were engaged, including Spitfires and Typhoons, among which three aircraft appeared to be hit.

As they pointed out, from their position in the anchorage, they had positively recognised the aircraft as friendly before a single shot was fired.

On the following day the Commander of Task Force 125 issued the following signal to all vessels in Utah area:

> No vessels other than man of war will fire at aircraft at any time unless under actual attack. Friendly 'planes have just been shot down. Withdrawal of protection will result from such practice. Any ship or craft which fired on any 'plane the late afternoon and evening of 9 June showed inexcusable ignorance and lack of good judgement.

Of another two Aircraft Identifiers, aboard the S.S. *John A. Sutter*, the Officer Commanding the U.S. Naval Armed Guard said:

> They have already proved worth their weight in gold to us in properly and quickly identifying all aircraft we have encountered in our initial invasion trip.
>
> As an example, on the morning of June 10th, with visibility poor, they caused us to hold our fire on two R.A.F. Spitfires which all other ships except Naval Units were firing at for a period of half an hour. When they reported aboard they told me they could identify anything they could see. Such has proved to be the case ...'

Many such reports were rendered both by Aircraft Identifiers and by the Officers under whom they served, both American and English, and those quoted above are only typical, in that they show both the general low standard of recognition, and the appreciation of the services of the trained Observers by the Masters of the Ships in which they served.

The Air Commander-in-Chief, A.E.A.F., in recording his appreciation, said: 'All reports agree that the seaborne volunteers have more than fulfilled their duties and have undoubtedly saved many of our aircraft from being engaged by ships' guns.'

In view of the numerous incidents during "Overlord" when friendly aircraft were destroyed or damaged by A.A. fire from ships (usually Naval) it was suggested by A.E.A.F. that:

(a) All ships should have trained aircraft identifiers who have no other responsibilities.
(b) A new trade of 'Aircraft Identifier' should be established by the Admiralty.
(c) While their training would be an Admiralty responsibility, R.O.C. personnel could be used as instructors.
(d) The Air Ministry should approach the Admiralty on those lines.

The matter of aircraft recognition was also taken up by the War Office on August 4th 1944, when the Under Secretary of State, Air Ministry, was asked for the services in Normandy of approximately 100 members of the R.O.C., who, it was suggested, would be stationed near the beaches when unloading was taking place. It was the intention that they should stop all A.A. fire by the firing of a recognised light signal. 'It will be realised', the letter continued, 'that the responsibility is a heavy one, and calls for greater expert recognition that can be provided by the army, including personnel of Anti-aircraft Command'.

In connection with this request, the Commandant, R.O.C., visited Normandy to find out exactly what was required by the 21 Army Group from whom the request had originated, but it was decided that the need for these Observers had now passed, and it was arranged instead to send out six experienced R.O.C. Officers to tour the A.A. sites and report to the Tactical Air Force (sending a copy of their report to the 21 Army Group) on the standard of recognition, with suggestions for its improvement.

Observer Captain V.O. Robinson O.B.E., M.C. of the Royal Observer Corps was then sent to France with six R.O.C. officers and eventually rendered a report on September 25th 1944 to the Commandant R.O.C. In it he commenced by saying that the 21st Army Group did not ask for a written report on the conclusion of the mission. However he gave the Commandant an account of discussions that took place with 21st Army Group and G.H.Q.A/A, and stated that it was the opinion both of 21st Army Group and of 2nd Tactical Air Force that the R.O.C. officers were really engaged in assisting individual units with their recognition training and a report coming from a separate service, whilst helpful, was not called for and, in fact, was inadvisable. The discussions really comprised a verbal report, the result of visits to, and interviews with, personnel, of some 65 different Units, Brigade Headquarters, Batteries or Troops.

The conclusions which he and his officers had reached was that there was, both in H.A.A. and L.A.A., a considerable variation of efficiency between the various units. This variation was due to three main reasons:

(i)   No standard was laid down.
(ii) No establishment of qualified aircraft identifiers existed.
(iii) Efficiency consequently varied with the attitude of the Commander of each individual unit to the subject. The opinion of the troops and battery commanders was the most important under the existing circumstances and organisation, and then that of the Regimental and Brigade commanders.

A very considerable knowledge of aircraft recognition existed but, owing to lack of standard establishment and qualifications and lack of status of the subject, also owing to inadequate organization of Regimental instructors and instructional material, that knowledge was quite haphazard in its distribution. Some fire units were very poor, others very bad and certainly likely to make mistakes.

A summary of recommendations was made, of which a copy was given to the officer representing G.H.Q.A/A Troops, and of which it is not necessary to give full details. The main suggestions comprised the laying down of a minimum establishment of qualified instructors, the provision of qualified identifiers in the lower formations (the actual fire units), recognised tests at regular intervals for their identifiers being a necessity. It was also recommended that instructional literature should be supplied, and that the instructional vans then in use should be replaced by larger type equipped with episcopes, film projectors and accommodation for a class of 8 to 12 persons.

Telling and Plotting Exercises – Discontinuation

With the invasion of Europe and the consequent shifting of the centre of activity from the British Isles it was decided that the R.O.C. Telling and Plotting Exercises, which had been introduced in 1939 to provide practice for both R.O.C. Tellers and R.A.F. Plotters, might be discontinued.

Conditions in both services had become more stable and, while in the more active operational areas sufficient activity prevailed to keep all personnel fully employed throughout the twenty-four hours, in the less active areas the reduced manning in force in R.A.F. Operations Rooms and the introduction of the Inland Multiphones made it impossible to carry out the exercises usefully. These exercises were, therefore, discontinued with effect from August 4th 1944.

Telling of Tracks by R.O.C. Centres – Reduced Manning

As mentioned above, manning in certain R.A.F. Operations Rooms had been put on a reduced standard, and it was therefore impossible to man continuously all plotting lines from R.O.C. Centres. A new procedure was therefore introduced in connection with the Operations Rooms concerned, and this procedure came into force on July 24th 1944.

The R.O.C. Centre was responsible for:

(i) Advising those Groups and Sectors with which it had liaison facilities, and to which it told, when a hostile unidentified or an S.O.S. track was originated by that Centre, or when a change of identification or the addition of S.O.S. necessitated the telling of a track not previously told.

(ii) Advising the same recipients when it commenced to tell hostile, unidentified or S.O.S. tracks which had been previously plotted either by Radar or by another R.O.C. Centre.

When this procedure had been adopted by the R.O.C. Centre it became then the responsibility of the Group or Sector concerned to ensure that the appropriate plotters' position was manned.

The procedure outlined above did not apply to the Operations Rooms at Headquarters Nos. 10 and 11 Fighter Groups and Coltishall, North Weald, Biggin Hill, Tangmere, Nether Wallop and Exeter R.A.F. Sectors, as these were fully manned. Similarly no warning of that nature was required to be given to Filter Rooms where the Inland Reporting Scheme was in operation, as their Inland Tables were continuously manned.

Chapter 11

The Stand-Down, The Past and The Future

Stand-down came for the Royal Observer Corps on May 12th 1945. For nearly six years, from August 24th 1939, Observer Centres and Posts had been manned for twenty-four hours in each day. From its small beginnings, in the years after the first World War, the Corps had grown by the end of 1944 to a total strength of over 32,000 of whom some 9,200 were employed full-time, the remainder carrying out their Observer Corps duties in the spare time left over from their civilian occupations. These figures included 4,300 women and girls of whom some 2,800 were employed full-time. While prior to 1937 only the Eastern and Southern Counties of England were covered by Observer Posts, by the end of the war some 1,400 Posts kept almost the entire sky over Great Britain under constant observation.

In addition to its main function of raid reporting and of giving assistance to the R.A.F. Flying Control organization in "homing" aircraft lost or in distress, the Corps had been directly incorporated in the Air Raid Warning System.

At the time of the invasion of Normandy some 800 Observers had been accepted and enrolled as aircraft identifiers on defensively equipped merchant ships, where high appreciation was shown of their skill by the commanders of both British and American ships.

With the developments that have taken place on raid reporting, and with the progress made by Radar, it is not possible as yet to picture the ultimate raid reporting systems. What seems certain is that for Royal Observer Corps the "stand-down" is not the end, and for some years to come their services will still be needed, skilled men ready at short notice to act again as "The Eyes and Ears of the Royal Air Force".

Appendices

144

Appendix I

Proposed Extension of the Observer Corps 1937

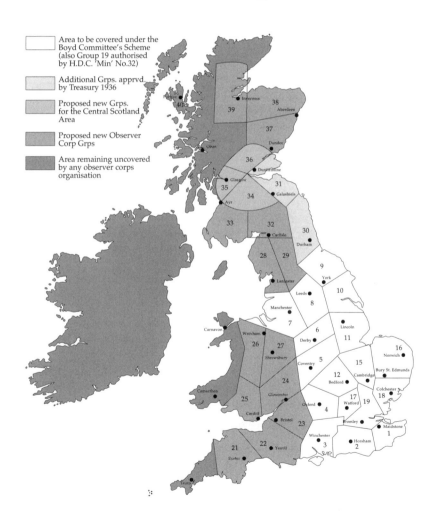

Area to be covered under the Boyd Committee's Scheme (also Group 19 authorised by H.D.C. 'Min' No.32)

Additional Grps. apprvd. by Treasury 1936

Proposed new Grps. for the Central Scotland Area

Proposed new Observer Corp Grps

Area remaining uncovered by any observer corps organisation

Appendix II

R.O.C. Areas and Groups
at Stand-Down 1945

Appendix III

Proposed Warning System

Proposed Warning System – C.I.D. 135-A. Schedule I. Paras.1-8

1. The warning system may be divided into two parts:
   (a) The collection of information regarding the enemy's activity; this is a Service responsibility.
   (b) The distribution of the information to the areas threatened. The issue of warnings is a Home Office responsibility, the Service authorities being responsible for transmitting the information in which any particular district is to receive the prearranged signals notifying the approach of hostile aircraft.

2. Information is collected:
   (a) From directional wireless and Admiralty sources.
   (b) From coastal watching centres, sound mirrors working seaward and other devices on the coast.
   (c) From observation zones, observation posts working through observation centres, as described in paragraph 3, et seq. below.
   (d) From the zones in which the air defences are operating, from anti-aircraft gun and searchlight stations, and from various listening devices.

3. The observation system 2(c) above is as follows:
   The whole land area that is considered to be within bombing range of a possible attack is divided into observation zones. Each zone is covered by a network of observer posts, one post

147

to every square of 6 or 7 miles side.

In each zone the observer posts are connected by direct telephone to an observation centre, where the courses of all hostile aircraft are plotted on a control map.

4. The posts and centre are manned by an Observer Corps of Special Constables: the organisation in each zone being under the direction of a controller. This controller would act under the authority of the Chief Constables of counties and boroughs in the matter of the provision of personnel; he would act under the authority of the G.O.C. Ground Troops in matters of technical training and in operations.

5. The members of the Observer Corps to be volunteers, enrolled as Special Constables, who undertake to carry out the observer work as a part of their constabulary duties. In some cases they may be enrolled for observer work only, and without acceptance of the general responsibilities of the Special Constabulary.

    The duties would be local, and numbers would incur no liability to carry out the observation work at a distance from their homes. In fact the scheme depends on their living within easy reach of their respective posts and centres.

6. The observation centres, of which, in present and near future conditions, there may be eighteen or twenty, would be connected by direct telephone lines to Fighting Area Headquarters and would transmit to the Headquarters control map courses of enemy aircraft.

    For all communications existing Post Office lines will be used, the only construction work required being the wiring of the Centres, and short extensions from local post offices to the actual observer posts in the open.

7. After a preliminary experiment in 1924, two zones have been organised in 1925. Zone No. 1, the whole of Kent, with 27 posts and a centre in Maidstone; Zone No. 2 East and West Sussex, with 16 posts, and a centre in Horsham.

    Tests, by day and night, with the co-operation of three

squadrons of the R.A.F., were carried out in June 1925. During the later tests the system was worked in with the coastal watching organisation and with a partial lay-out of Fighting Area Headquarters.

The work in the two zones was very successful; a large number of simultaneous courses, many of a complicated nature, have been accurately and rapidly plotted on the control maps.

The special constables, who were carefully selected by the Chief Constables, proved very keen and efficient at the work.

8. It is now proposed to give the Observer Corps a permanent standing, so that the system may be brought into action at short notice, either for practice or in an emergency.

    It is further proposed in 1926 to organise observation zones in Hampshire and the Eastern Counties; when this is done, the more likely lines of approach on London itself will be covered. As soon as each zone has been organised and has received the necessary initial instruction, it is intended to hand it over to the Zone Controller, as outlined above (in paragraph 4).

Appendix IV

Duties of the Raids Intelligence Officer and the Observer Corps Liaison Officer

DUTIES OF THE RAIDS INTELLIGENCE OFFICER
1. A Raids Intelligence Officer is located in each Fighter Group Operations Room in such a position as gives him a good view of the plotting table.
2. The Raids Intelligence Officer is responsible for the Fighter Group table procedure and for the direction of the floor. For this purpose he will have direct communication with the Floor Supervisor.
3. Under the directions of the Group Controller he will be responsible for the allocation of raid or X numbers to tracks 'Told' by Observer Centres with an Observer Centre letter and number and will inform the O.C.L.O. and Floor Supervisor of the raid or X number allocated.
4. He will receive particulars of missing raids from the Recorder.
5. He is to estimate the probable position of the lost raid and pass the information to the O.C.L.O. who will make enquiries from the Observer Corps Centre.
6. If a raid is given by an Observer Corps Centre at or near the estimated position, the Raids Intelligence Officer in conjunction with the Observer Corps Liaison Officer will decide whether this is in fact the missing raid, and if this is so the Raids Intelligence Officer will duly inform the Observer Corps Liaison Officer.
7. If requested by the O.C.L.O., when unable to do so himself, he should communicate direct with the Observer Centre or

Centres concerned in order to obtain first-hand information from the Controller of the Centre regarding the missing raid.

8. If a raid is found and the R.I.O. is able to identify the track with a missing raid, the correct number will be allotted by the quickest means possible. If this identification is not possible, one of the special numbers allotted to the Group concerned will be given by the R.I.O.

DUTIES OF THE OBSERVER CORPS LIAISON OFFICER

1. A Liaison Officer is located in each Fighter Group Operations Room in such a position as gives him a good view of the plotting table.

2. He has a switchboard through which he can speak to the Controllers of all Observer Centres which 'Tell' to that Fighter Group, and to the Fighter Group Operations Officer.

3. His duties are:

   (i)   To watch the tracking of raids on the potting table, and, when these become disconnected or indeterminate, to check the 'Telling' by communicating with the Controller of the Centre concerned. When a numbered or X track has appeared on the Fighter Group table the permission of the Group Controller must be obtained before any instructions are given to the Centre to cease 'Telling'.

   (ii)   To ensure as far as possible that tracks and their numbers are taken over from the R.D.F. and carried on from Centre to Centre.

   (iii)   To assist in the finding of lost raids. If the O.C.L.O. is fully occupied when a raid is lost, he should ask the R.I.O. to communicate with the Centre or Centres of the Observer Group area it is estimated to have reached.

   (iv)   When an Observer Centre 'Tells' a track with Observer Centre letter and number, the O.C.L.O. should at once ask the R.I.O. for a raid or X number and inform the Centre of the number allotted. When an Observer Centre reports an unidentified track, the O.C.L.O. will ask the Group Controller if the track is to be 'Told'. If the reply is in the affirmative, the O.C.L.O. will obtain a number from the R.I.O. and inform the Centre.

(v) If the O.C.L.O. observes that the information displayed on the Group table differs from that being transmitted from the Observer Centre he will inform the R.I.O. The O.C.L.O. will not give orders to the Floor Supervisor.

(vi) To pass orders from Observer Corps Commandant, or the Fighter Group, to the Centres concerned.

(vii) To watch the state of "readiness" of all the Observer Groups in his Fighter Group area.

(viii)To pass on to the Fighter Group any information of interest received from Centres, including reports of bombs dropped, aircraft crashes, dropping of parachutes, and also events at sea seen by Observer Posts, such as the sighting of enemy submarines, the dropping of mines by aircraft, casualties to vessels or aircraft, etc.

Appendix V

Memoranda Nos. 1, 2 and 3

MEMORANDUM No.1: RE-ORGANISATION OF R.O.C. AREAS

1. *Information*
(a)   R.O.C. Areas now conform territorially with Fighter Groups. The removal of all Area Headquarters to Fighter Group Headquarters will be completed by the end of 1942.
(b)   The establishment of R.O.C. Area Headquarters is at present an Area Commandant and two Deputy Commandants who divide between them geographically the Observer Groups for which they are responsible. The administrative staff consists of an Administrative Officer whose duties are largely concerned with questions of pay and personnel, and an Equipment Officer. There are five permanent R.O.C.L.O's at each Fighter Group and one reserve R.O.C.L.O.

2. *Recommendations*
(a)   I recommend that the establishment of one Deputy Commandant be abolished, the remaining Deputy to be charged with Operations and training. In addition this officer would from time to time assist the R.O.C.L.O's in their duties.
(b)   It is further recommended that the number of R.O.C.L.O's at each Fighter Group be reduced to four.
(c)   In view of the proposed training scheme it is desirable that an Operations Staff Officer be appointed, principally for the purpose of supervising the training of R.O.C. Post and Centre personnel.

(d) It is suggested that this Area Training Officer be paid at the rate of £400 per annum.

(e) is recommended that an Adjutant be appointed at each Area Headquarters at a salary of £300 per annum.

(f) Addendum A shews in diagram the changes involved in this re-organisation of Area Headquarters.

(g) Addendum B shews the relative cost of the existing arrangement and of the proposed arrangement.

Addendum A: Proposed Re-Organisation of ROC Area Headquarters
Addendum B: Establishments

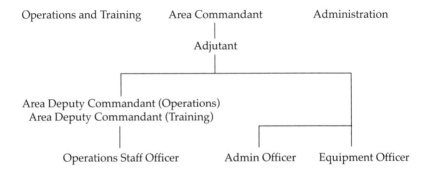

EXISTING

Unit	Establishments	Salary	No. of Units	Total Establishments	Total Cost
Areas	1 Area Commandant	£650	6	6 Area Commandants	£3,900
	2 D/Area Commandants	£550		12 D/Area Commandants	£6,600
	5 ROCLOs	£425		30 ROCLOs	£12,750
	1 Equipment Officer	£350		6 Equipment Officers	£2,100
	1 Admin Officer	£400		6 Admin Officers	£2,400

Total No. of Officers per Area HQ 10
Total Cost per Area HQ £27,750

PROPOSED

Unit	Establishments	Salary	No. of Units	Total Establishments	Total Cost
Areas	1 Area Commandant	£650	6	6 Area Commandants	£3,900
	1 D/Area Commandants	£550		6 D/Area Commandants	£3,300
	1 Operations Staff Officer	£400		6 Ops. Staff Officer	£2,400
	4 ROCLOs	£425		24 ROCLOs	£10,200
	1 Equipment Officer	£350		6 Equipment Officers	£2,100
	1 Admin Officer	£400		6 Admin Officers	£2,400
	1 Adjutant	£300		6 Adjutants	£1,800

Total No. of Officers per Area HQ   10
Total Cost per Area HQ   £26,100

MEMORANDUM No.2: RE-ORGANISATION OF R.O.C. GROUPS

1. *Information*
(a) The present organisation of the R.O.C. Groups is one of the main obstacles to smooth operational and administrative working in the R.O.C. At present a system of dual control is in force. The Centre Controller is responsible for the Operations Room while the Observer Group Officer is responsible for the Posts which supply information to the Operations Room. These two officers are equal in command and status.
(b) In the absence of any officer to assume responsibility for both Posts and Centres there is an inevitable division of effort, lack of liaison, and consequent inefficiency. Controversial matters, which often owe their origin to this division in the Group, have to be referred to an Area Deputy Commandant. Under the present system the harmonious working between Centre and Posts on which depends the general operational efficiency of the Group is often notable

by its absence. The changes in organisation which I recommend are designed to give a greater cohesion and unity to the R.O.C. Group.

2. *Recommendations*
(a) I recommend that a Group Commandant be appointed who will be responsible for both Posts and Centre in the R.O.C. Group.
(b) It is suggested that the pay of the Group Commandant should be at the rate of £500 per annum.
(c) The Group Commandant to be assisted by an Adjutant with pay at the rate of £300 per annum.
(d) The post of Controller to be retained at the present salary of £400 per annum, but that of Deputy Controller to be abolished. The Controller to act as Deputy Group Commandant.
(e) I recommend that the rank of Duty Controller be up graded to that of Officer in view of his heavy operational responsibilities, which correspond not with those of the Head Observer with whom he is at present graded, but with those of the A.O.G.O.
(f) It is suggested that Duty Controllers be paid at the rate of £300 per annum. When their service is full-time service.
(g) It is recommended that the existing post of O.G.O. be abolished and the number of A.O.G.O's increased to a maximum of one per ten Posts. These officers will be directly responsible to the Group Commandant for the operational efficiency of their sections of Posts. These operational duties are laid down in paragraph 3.B. of memorandum No. 3.
(h) The proposed re-organisation of the Groups is shown diagrammatically at Addendum C. The cost of this scheme relative to the present organisation is at Addendum D.

3. *Conclusion*
If authority is given for the proposals set out in this memorandum it is not proposed to implement them forthwith, but only as and when the changes are deemed to be expedient. Certain groups are ready for an immediate change, in others considerations such

as the finding of suitable personnel to fill the proposed new appointments are likely to cause delay.

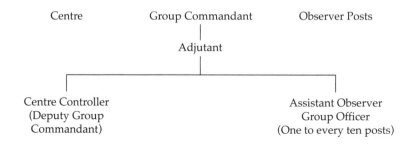

Addendum C: Proposed Re-Organisation of ROC Group Headquarters

Addendum D: Establishments

Unit	Establishments	Salary	No. of Units	Total Establishments	Total Cost
Group 1	OGO	£400	39	39 OGOs	£15,600
	1 Controller	£400	39	39 Controllers	£15,600
	3 AOGOs	£300	39	117 AOGOs	£35,100
	3½ D/Controllers	£270	39	137 D/Controllers	£36,990
					£103,290

PROPOSED

Unit	Establishments	Salary	No. of Units	Total Establishments	Total Cost
Group 1	Group Commandant	£500	39	39 Group Commandants	£19,500
	1 Controller	£400	39	39 Controllers	£15,600
	1 AOGO per 10 posts	£300	39	147 AOGOs	£44,100
	1 Adjutant	£300	39	39 Adjutants	£11,700
	3½ D/Controllers	£300	39	137 D/Controllers	£41.100
					£132,000

MEMORANDUM No.3: TRAINING OF R.O.C. POST
PERSONNEL

1. *Information*
No organised system of training R.O.C. Post personnel exists
at the present time in the R.O.C.

2. *Intention*
(a) To institute and carry out a comprehensive system of
training of R.O.C. Post personnel which will include
instruction in:
(1) Post Procedure.
(2) Standing Orders and Current Instructions.
(3) Aircraft Recognition.
(b) To establish a minimum standard of efficiency in Post
Procedure and Aircraft Recognition. Every Post Observer,
with certain reservations, will be obliged to reach and
maintain this standard.
(c) To organise a series of tests of varying standards in Aircraft
Recognition.

3. *Execution*
(a) Organisation.
(i)   R.O.C. Headquarters. There is an officer at R.O.C.
Headquarters responsible for the organisation of
training Post personnel throughout the R.O.C.
(ii) Area Headquarters. The Operations Staff Officer at
Area Headquarters will be the officer responsible for
training.
(iii) Groups. The A.O.G.O's are to be directly responsible to
the Group Commandant for organising all training and
instruction in their section of Posts.
(b) Duties of A.O.G.O.
(i)   He will be held responsible for the Operational
efficiency of his Posts.
(ii) A minimum of 10 Posts and a maximum of 12 Posts is
to be the basis of allotting a section of Posts to
A.O.G.O's.

(iii) The A.O.G.O's must visit each of his section of Posts at least once a week, and these visits are to include a visit during the hours of darkness to each of his section of Posts at least once a month.

(iv) These visits are normally to last a minimum of three hours and the A.O.G.O. is on occasions to perform duties of all his Posts.

(v) The A.O.G.O. is to be responsible for the selection of his Post Instructors and their efficiency.

(vi) The A.O.G.O. is to attend as many Post Meetings as possible. He should find it possible to attend a minimum of three meetings per week. At these meetings the A.O.G.O. will take charge and give a certain amount of Instruction himself and supervise any instruction given by the Post Instructor.

(vii) The A.O.G.O. will be held responsible for the distribution of all Aircraft Recognition material to his Posts.

(c) Duties of Post Instructors.

(i) Post Instructors will be responsible to their A.O.G.O. for conducting the training of their Post.

(ii) The P.I. is to be officially appointed to instruct all members of his Post in Post Procedure, Standing and Current Orders and Aircraft Recognition.

(iii) He will be responsible for the extra care and maintenance of all Aircraft Recognition material supplied to his Post including the indexing of all A.P. 1480 publications and the insertion of all amendments.

(iv) In the absence of the A.O.G.O. the P.I. is to take charge and instruct at all Post Meetings which will be held approximately once a week.

(d) Rank of Post Instructor.

The Post Instructor will be known as "Leading Observer" and (when not the Post Head Observer) will be entitled to wear two stripes on his uniform denoting his rank.

[Point 4 not included]

5. *Supply of Instructors*

(a) A.O.G.O.s.

    (i)   It is now compulsory for all A.O.G.O's who have not already passed one of the Instructor's Courses in the Isle of Man to attend and pass a new series of Instructor's Courses now being held in the Isle of Man.

    (ii) These courses are of three weeks duration. The R.O.C. has an allotment of 8 vacancies per course.

    (iii) As the allotting of Posts to A.O.G.O's has been based on a minimum of 10, and maximum of 12 Posts, approximately 30 A.O.G.O's additional to the present establishment of 117 will be required.

    (iv) A definite age limit of 50 has been laid down for all future appointments of A.O.G.O's.

6. *Post Meetings*

These are to be held once a week and will normally last an hour and a half.

7. *Tests*

(a) All Tests must be conducted by the A.O.G.O. responsible for any particular Post, and the written part of any Test should normally be conducted at the weekly Post Meetings held in his section.

(b) It is desirable to institute three separate Tests for R.O.C. Post personnel.

    (i)   Basic Test.

    (ii) Intermediate Aircraft Recognition Test.

    (iii) Master Test in Aircraft Recognition.

8. *Basic Tests*

(a) The standard to be aimed at in this Test is to be the minimum any Post Observer should be required to know concerning Post Procedure, Standing and Current Orders and Aircraft Recognition.

(b) The standard laid down is a standard below which no Post Observer should be given Operational Duty. If he fails to pass the basic test he should be replaced by a more competent Observer, as and when opportunity occurs.

(c) The Basic Test can be taken by members as opportunity offers, but must be taken by all Post Observers at least once every six months.

(d) The Basic Test will include:-

    (i)   Practical and Oral examination at the Post site on the working of the Observer instrument.

    (ii)   Written examination of Standing and Current Orders, as they effect Post Observers.

    (iii) A written test on approximately 50 Operational Friendly and Hostile Aircraft – (Silhouettes and Descriptions).

(e) In order to pass, Observers will have to obtain 80%.

9. *Intermediate Aircraft Recognition Test*

(a)   This Test will not be compulsory, but all Post Observers will be encouraged to take this Test.

(b)   Only those Post Observers who have passed the Basic Test during the previous six months will be eligible to take the Intermediate Test.

(c)   The A.O.G.O. is to arrange to hold an intermediate test whenever there is sufficient demand from any one of his Posts.

(d)   The Test will cover approximately 100 aircraft. Silhouettes will form half the Test, and Photographs (Flying views) will form the other half.

(e)   In order to pass, Observers will have to obtain 85%.

10. *Master Test in Aircraft Recognition*

(a)   This Test will not be compulsory and those passing the Master Test will be considered to have attained a high state of efficiency in Aircraft Recognition.

(b)   Only those Post Observers who have passed both the Basic and Intermediate Test during the previous six months will be eligible to take the Master Test.

(c)   In order to pass the Master Test, Observers will have to obtain 90%.

11. *Existing Post Test (Aircraft Recognition)*

(a)   For some six months past R.O.C. Posts in Northern and

Midland Areas have been issued with monthly sheets showing 21 Aircraft Photographs (Flying views) the Post solution being forwarded to Area Headquarters. This scheme which had recently been extended to include North-Western Area has proved extremely popular and it is hoped to extend it to other areas.

(b) The work of correcting results and compiling records of this Test is at the moment being undertaken by two ladies at Mr. Tapp's office. It is suggested that this Test be taken over by the R.O.C. and that Mr. Tapp and the organisers of the scheme be paid as part-time members of the R.O.C.

12. *Visits to Centres by Post Personnel*
(a) Periodical visits to their Centre is an important part of the training of Post Observers.
(b) All Post personnel will be required to visit their centre once every six months.

13. *Inter Post Visits and Inter-Post Competitions*
(a) Competitions in Aircraft Recognition between Posts and Groups of Posts help very considerably to stimulate enthusiasm by facilitating the exchange of ideas and an understanding of common difficulties.
(b) It is proposed to allow and encourage clusters of Posts (i.e. those Posts on the same telephone circuit) to meet together once every three months with the object of holding inter-cluster competitions in Aircraft Recognition.
(c) It is further proposed that the winners of the inter-cluster competitions be allowed to meet once every six months with the object of holding a Group competition in Aircraft Recognition.
(d) It may be desired to extend this further by the winning teams from each Group, within an Area, meeting together for an Area competition on similar lines.

14. *Badges*
It is proposed that a proficiency badge in the form of a woven Spitfire be awarded to those Observers who have passed the Master Test in Aircraft Recognition.

15. *Equipment*
M.A.P. have undertaken the supply of all Aircraft recognition material for the R.O.C.

16. *Cost of Instructors*

A.O.G.O. Approximately 30 additional A.O.G.O's will be required at £300 per annum: £9,000. 0s. 0d.

Post Instructors Number required 1402 with a responsibility allowance of 10s/- per week: £36,452. 0s. 0d.

Addendum
With the introduction of the training scheme a certain amount of additional travelling will result, involving the use of private transport and the payment of 1d. per mile allowance to Post Observers living more than two miles from the place of instructions.

The times that the above conditions will apply are:

1. Weekly Post Meetings.
2. Inter Post Meetings every three months.
3. Inter group Meetings every six months.
4. Visits to R.O.C. Centres twice per year.

It is not possible to give an exact estimate of the cost of travelling and the petrol involved but it is estimated that the total will not exceed 1/7th of the present total in either case.

Against the use of public transport mentioned above must be put the consumption of petrol and use of private transport that arose in the past owing to the activities of the R.O.C. Club. The monthly allowance of petrol for Club purposes is 1,500 gallons.

Appendix VI

Recommendations Regarding the Increased Commitments of the R.O.C

From: Headquarters, Royal Observer Corps.

To: Headquarters, Fighter Command.

Ref: ROC/S. 117/Air.

Date: 30th December, 1942.

SUBJECT: RECOMMENDATIONS REGARDING THE INCREASED COMMITMENTS OF THE ROYAL OBSERVER CORPS.

1. *Duties of the R.O.C. at the Beginning of the War*
(a) When the system was designed and at first operated, the functions of the R.O.C. were briefly as follows:
   (i) Posts. To report the position of aircraft continuously to the R.O.C. Centre and co-operate in this duty with those Posts on the same telephone circuit. Aircraft Recognition as it is now understood was not the official duty of the Observers on the Posts.
   (ii) Centres. To "Tell" required tracks of friendly aircraft and all hostile and unidentified aircraft simultaneously to a Fighter Group and Sector Operations Room. The reporting of crashes and other unusual incidents to the Groups and Sectors was also the responsibility of the Centre.

(b) Communications to cover these duties were provided between:-
   (i)   Post and Centre.
   (ii) Centre and Centre.
   (iii) Centre and Fighter Operations Rooms.
(c) It should be noted that there have been no increases in communications to this framework, which is the structure of the system, since the war began.

2. *Duties Subsequently Added Since the Beginning of the War*
(a) Posts.
   (i) Aircraft Recognition.
   (ii) The receiving of plots of aircraft from Coastguard Stations and liaison with Coastguard Stations. Direct lines have been provided between Coastguard Stations and 129 Coastal Posts for this purpose.
   (iii) The receiving of information from Satellite Posts connected by direct telephone to a Post. There are three kinds of satellites, which are manned only in daylight, as under:
   R.O.C. Satellite Posts. (27) (A Post manned by a single R.O.C. Observer).
   A.A. Command Searchlight Sites. (50) (A line from the Sentry to the R.O.C. Post is required).
   Aerodrome Lookouts. (22) (A direct line to the nearest R.O.C. Post is required).
   The policy is to provide such types of satellite Posts within a 30 mile belt of the South Coast, East Coast as far as Dundee and on the coast of Lancashire and Cheshire.
   (iv) The relaying of Air Raid Alarms to factories engaged on war production on the instruction of the Ministry of Home Security Alarm Controllers situated in the Centres. The Alarm is passed from the Post to the factory either by speech line or a press button sounding a buzzer at the factory. It should be noted that when an Alarm Controller passes the instruction for the Post to give the warning the original Post circuit is used and this interferes with the working of the plotter and the other Posts on the same circuit.

(v) The issue of direct Air Raid Warnings by 31 Posts on the South Coast direct to the Siren Control point. Such warnings are issued by the Observer on his own initiative when he has seen and recognised an enemy aircraft. After issuing such a warning the Observer has to report this to the Plotter at the Centre who informs the Alarm Controller. In addition, the Observer has to report when he hears the Siren sounded. It is pointed out that these messages occupy Posts circuits at the very time when all the Posts on the circuit should be reporting the enemy aircraft to the Centre.

(vi) The operation of the Schumurly rocket when low flying enemy aircraft have been seen and recognised. The rocket apparatus is installed at 69 Coastal Posts on the South Coast.

(vii) The operation of Darky R/T sets for the homing of lost friendly aircraft. At present 16 Posts are fitted and 29 scheduled to be fitted with R/T sets and though this required additional knowledge on the part of the Observer the operation of the sets does not necessarily synchronise with enemy activity and this does not, therefore affect operationally the normal function of the Post.

(viii) The operation of searchlights installed or about to be installed at 107 Posts for the homing of lost friendly aircraft. It should be noted that two extra Observers have to be on duty at night for this purpose and though the operation of searchlights does not directly affect the efficiency of the Post the men required have to be drawn from the normal Post personnel.

(ix) The reporting of aircraft showing distress signals.

(x) The operation of G.L.'s at 10 Posts.

(xi) The passing of messages originated by the Army, if engaged on anti-invasion operations.

(xii) The issuing of warnings to Home Guard detachments and Commanders by direct telephone lines.

(xiii) The issuing of unofficial Air Raid Warnings to Bomber Stations and other interested authorities who have secured direct lines to the Post by local arrangements.

(b) Centres.
- (i)   The immediate reporting of bombs and flares to Fighter Groups for onward transmission to Fighter Command.
- (ii) Reports of Air Raid Warnings originated by Posts to be passed to the Air Raid Warning Officer at Group.
- (iii) The relaying of messages by plotters between the Alarm Controller and Posts in regard to Air Raid Warnings and Alarm warnings to Factories.
- (iv) G.L. Interrogation.
- (v)   Air Raid Warnings to Bomber Groups, Bomber Stations and many other authorities.
- (vi) Liaison and passing of tracks by direct telephone line to A.A. Command, Gun Operations Rooms. The direct lines in the instances where this arrangement is in force have been supplied by local arrangement.
- (vii) Liaison in regard to aircraft in distress direct to Bomber Groups, Bomber Stations and O.T.U.'s by direct lines. Mainly provided by local arrangement. Liaison with the Regional Commissioner, Police and many other local arrangements covering generally Air Raid Warnings.

3. *Comments*

(a) It will be seen from the above paragraph that the duties of the R.O.C. generally have increased immeasurably since the beginning of the war. Very many of these increased commitments have been added from time to time without relation to each other. Many of them are the result of direct local arrangement and have involved the provision in many cases of direct telephone lines.

(b) It is considered that the time has come when it is necessary to review all these commitments in the light of operational requirements and shortage of man-power and telephone lines. It is felt that the increasing complexity caused is slowing down the operation of the Royal Observer Corps generally. It should be noted that many of these increased commitments have been undertaken during a period of comparatively slight enemy activity with the result that the essential function of the R.O.C., that is, the immediate reporting of enemy aircraft to action-taking authorities, has for this reason been jeopardised.

(c) Many of the commitments undertaken may be found to be useful and necessary and it felt that the mass of information existing in R.O.C. Centres should be made available to those authorities requiring the information but that a line should be drawn between those authorities requiring information, and those who want it purely for interest. Having decided which authorities should have the information, then it is considered that a rationalized and standard method of broadcast to those authorities would result in greater efficiency and probably a saving in man-power and telephone lines.

(d) One thing is certain that the original principle in the functioning of the Observer Corps should be re-established, in that the Posts should be responsible for obtaining information and forwarding to the Centres, and Centres should be responsible for the broadcast of the information. Posts should never be required to forward information to any party other than the Centre to which it is connected, (with the exception of shipping reports to Coastguards).

4. *Recommendations*
(a) Connection between Coastguard Stations and R.O.C. Posts.

    (i)   129 Posts are connected by direct telephone lines to Coastguard Stations. The reason for such connection is to provide for general exchange of information between Coastguard and Coastal R.O.C. Posts. Sometimes R.O.C. Posts are able to report shipping to Coastguards. This does not affect the operational efficiency of the Post and may help the Coastguard Stations considerably. Sometimes the sound of motor boats may be mistaken by the Royal Observer Corps for an aircraft and in case of doubt reference to the Coastguard may clear this point.

    (ii)   One object of the line between Coastguards and R.O.C. Posts is to enable Coastguards to pass plots of aircraft flying out over the sea to the R.O.C. Posts and thereby helping to increase the coastwise coverage. It is considered that the connections between Coastguards and R.O.C. Posts should be left intact.

(b) Satellite Posts.

   (i)   It is confidently believed that the policy for the provision of Satellite Posts laid down in the letter reference FC/S. 25333 dated 14th March, 1942, is unlikely to provide any benefit commensurate with the outlay in human and communication resources.

  (ii)   To make the Royal Observer Corps coverage proof even within 30 miles of the sea coast from low flying single enemy aircraft is absolutely impossible within practicable limits. To do so would require posts spaced something like ½ mile intervals which is outside the bounds of possibility.

 (iii)   To provide 150 Satellite Posts even within a 30 mile belt of the coast could only improve the coverage by very small fractions. Against this addition must be laid the increased delay in communications caused by the fact that they are connected by direct telephone each to one Post which in itself already shares a circuit with 2 or 3 other Posts. Thus the communications to the Centre of some 500 Coastal Posts are likely to be adversely affected.

 (iv)   It is considered that the problem of gaps in the coverage should be tackled in only two ways, either by the re-siting of an existing Post, or, if possible, by the provision of a new complete Post with normal communications. If after this action the gaps still exist then they should be accepted and emphasis laid on ensuring maximum speed in the transmission of plots in these instances when an enemy aircraft is seen by a Post.

  (v)   It is going to be of little use if a few more enemy aircraft are seen by the Post but delay in transmission of plots is increased.

 (vi)   It is, therefore, recommended that the policy requiring provision of Satellite Posts be completely abandoned.

(c) Post Communication.

   (i)   It is recommended that no Post should be permitted to have more than one line additional to the normal Post circuit to the Centre and that this line, if provided, should be to a Coastguard. Warnings to factories or Coastal Towns should be operated by a press button in the R.O.C. Post.

(d) Gun Operations Rooms.

    (i)   A.A. Command have asked that many R.O.C. Centres should have direct lines to Gun Operations Rooms. The provision of these lines was held up pending the advent of Inland Reporting.

    (ii) It is recommended that Fighter Command should give a ruling on this matter and that if it is eventually decided that Gun Operations Rooms require information from R.O.C. Centre Rooms then the lines should be connected to the R.O.C. tellers and information should be broadcast to the Gun Operations Room in exactly a similar manner to the method used for broadcast to Sectors and Groups.

(e) Bomber Groups and Stations.

    (i)   Air Ministry have under consideration a scheme for passing plots from R.O.C. Centres to Bomber Groups. The idea behind this scheme is to give the Bomber Groups information in the form of plots of enemy intruder aircraft. This scheme requires that the Bomber Groups should become customers of the R.O.C. and receive information similarly from the teller as do Sectors and Fighter Groups.

    (ii) It is recommended that if this scheme is accepted all existing lines and arrangements between R.O.C. Centres and Bomber Groups and Stations should be withdrawn.

(f) Other authorities requesting information.

    (i)   It is recommended that Fighter Command should make a ruling as to which authorities (possibly, Training Command Groups, Coast Command Groups) are to receive information from R.O.C. Centres and, after this ruling has been made, that no unofficial arrangements should be made either locally or otherwise without the permission of Fighter Command.

    (ii) It is recommended that the broadcast of information from R.O.C. centres to any authorities approved by

Fighter Command should be on the same lines as the scheme now under consideration for Bomber Groups, in other words all recipients of information from R.O.C. Centres should become customers just like Sectors and Fighter Groups.

(g) Aircraft in Distress.

(i) At the present time some R.O.C. Centres with lines to Bomber Groups and Stations are giving direct assistance in regard to aircraft in distress. This must cause considerable overlapping because the Flying Control Liaison Officer in the Fighter Group may be taking certain action in regard to a distress Bomber, and the Bomber Station through its direct contact with the R.O.C. Centre may be taking quite different action. Cases of this kind have already occurred.

(ii) Now that the Flying Control organisation is built up and functioning it is recommended that all reports of aircraft in distress and any reference to them should be made by the R.O.C. Centre direct to the Flying Control Liaison Officer in the Fighter Group and that no action should be taken direct with any other authority.

These recommendations are made following a Day Operations Conference held on the 17th December, 1942. (With reference to Minutes FC/S. 29715 dated 18th December, 1942).

(Sgd.) G.H. Ambler
Air Commodore
Commandant, Royal Observer Corps

Appendix VII

Memoranda Nos. 4 and 5

Memorandum No.4: Re-Organisation of Centre Crews

Information

1. At the present time the responsibility for the efficient working of a Centre crew is vested in the Duty Controller who has four assistants to help him in the discharge of these duties:-

(i) The Duty Controller's assistant who sits beside the Duty Controller and is supposed to assist him in any of his multitudinous duties.

(ii) The Sector Liaison Teller who is responsible for maintaining Liaison with the Sectors.

(iii) The R.O.C. Sector Liaison Teller who is situated inside the Sector Operations Room and mans the telephone line and so works with the Sector Liaison Teller in the R.O.C. Centre.

(iv) The Table Supervisor who is responsible for supervising the Plotters around the main table, and also for the provision of raid plaques as required by the Plotters.

2. This has been the organisation of a crew since the beginning of the war, with the exception that the R.O.C. Liaison Teller in the Sectors is a recent provision which has proved most satisfactory to Fighter Command.

3. Since the beginning of the war there has been a vast increase, not only in the operational responsibilities thrust upon the Duty

Controller but also in extra duties, so that now it is quite impossible for the Duty Controller to carry out what is expected of him unless there is some devolution of responsibilities and duties to those Observers working under him.

4. This devolution has in some cases taken place, but in rather a general way, in that there is no strict definition of particular duties or responsibilities for the four assistants quoted in paragraph 1. (i), (ii), (iii) and (iv).

Proposals
5. It is considered that it is now necessary to define the duties and responsibilities delegated to the key Observers in R.O.C. Centres, to prevent overlapping and confusion which is taking place at the present time. Coincident with the defining if individual responsibilities it is also proposed to give appropriate ranks in keeping with the responsibilities devolved on each individual. The proposed duties of the Observers are set out below:

(i) *The Duty Controller*. This Observer has already been upgraded of officer status. Broadly his duties and responsibilities will be as follows:

(a) He will be responsible for the efficiency of the Centre crew and the efficient working of the whole Group controlled from that Centre during his tour of duty. This includes the responsibility for the efficient working of all the Posts feeding that Centre.

(b) He will, in fact, represent the Group Commandant during the time that he, the Duty Controller, is on duty.

(c) He will be responsible for working with the R.O.C.L.O. on duty at the Fighter Group and for carrying out the instructions passed to him from the Fighter Group Controller through the R.O.C.L.O.

(d) It will be seen, therefore, that operationally his functions fall into two classes, firstly he is responsible for the input of information into the R.O.C. Centre and secondly, for the output of information to Fighter Group, Sectors, and other Air Force authorities. It is proposed that he should hold one Observer responsible for each of these two functions.

(ii) *Post Controller.* An Observer holding this position is at present known as Duty Controller's Assistant and, as previously stated, his duties are ill-defined. Under the present proposals his duties will be broadly as follows:-

(a) He will be responsible for the input of information from Posts to the Centre.

(d) He will be responsible for the taking over of tracks of aircraft flying from one R.O.C. Group into his R.O.C. Group.

(c) As all the Posts on one telephone circuit and the Plotter for those Posts must be considered as one unit, the Post Controller will be held equally responsible for the efficient collaboration of both Post Observers and Plotters during his tour of duty.

(d) The Post Controller will be provided with a keyboard which will permit him to listen in to any Post circuit at any time and speak to any Post Observer or any Plotter. It will be seen, therefore, that under this arrangement both the Observers at a Post and the Plotters in the Centre serving them, will be under the constant supervision of the Post Controller. The placing of both Plotters and Post Observers under one operational authority at all times should do a great deal to smooth out friction at present existing between post observer and plotters in the Centre.

(e) It is emphasised, that the duties of the Post Controller will be confined entirely to the input of information for which he will be held responsible by the Duty Controller.

(iii) *Assistant Duty Controller.* The proposed Assistant Duty Controller is at present known as the Sector Liaison Teller and his present duties are confined to liaison with the Sectors. Under these proposals his duties will be broadly as follows:-

(a) He will be held responsible by the Duty Controller for the output of information from the Centre to connected R.A.F. authorities.

(b) He will be held responsible for the efficient working of the Tellers in the R.O.C. Centre.

(c) He will be responsible for liaison with the R.O.C. Liaison Tellers situated in the Sector Operations Rooms.

(d) In the absence of the Duty Controller he will also work with the R.O.C. Liaison Officer in the Fighter Group, and assume the responsibilities of the Duty Controller.

(iv) *R.O.C. Liaison Tellers in the Fighter Sectors*. Both the name and the duties of these individuals will remain unchanged under the new proposals. The provision of R.O.C. Observers in the Fighter Sector Operations Rooms has proved a very great success, and it is considered that these individuals are now occupying a position of some responsibility.

(v) *Floor Supervisor*. The proposed Floor Supervisor is at present known as Table Supervisor and his responsibilities are mainly concerned with the efficient working of the plotters. In some cases he is expected to supervise the Post Observers but as he has no telephone facilities to speak to the Observers this function is a difficult one to carry out. Under the new proposals his duties and responsibilities will be as follows:-

(a) To supervise the arrangements for the provision of raid plaques, counters etc., to Plotters requirements.

(b) The discipline of all persons employed in the well on the lower floor of the Centre Operations Room.

(c) He will work directly under the Duty Controller and will also take instructions from the Post Controller.

Proposed Ranks

6.　(i) Approval has already been obtained for Duty Controllers to hold the rank of Observer Officer.

(ii) *Post Controller*. It is suggested that the Post Controller should hold the rank of Chief Observer. This rank would then correspond to that held by the Head Observer in charge of each Post. It is considered absolutely necessary that the Post Controller should hold this rank which should enable him to exercise supervision over the Observers on duty at the Posts. The responsibilities of a Post Controller will be very considerable and he will occupy a position in the R.O.C.

Centre similar to that of a Filter Officer in the R.A.F. Filter Rooms.

(iii) *Assistant Duty Controllers.* It is suggested that the Assistant Duty Controller should also hold the rank of Chief Observer. In the course of his duties he will have to supervise the Tellers in the R.O.C. Centre and be held generally responsible for the output of information, equivalent to that of the Post Controller on the input side. He will assume the responsibilities of Duty Controller in the absence of that officer.

(iv) *R.O.C. Liaison Teller in the Fighter Command Sector Operations Room.* It is proposed that this Observer should be upgraded to the rank of Chief Observer. He is the R.O.C. representative in the Fighter Sector Operations Room, and therefore, holds a post of considerable responsibility. In addition, to this, these Observers are now accommodated in the Sergeants Mess at R.A.F. Stations and it is, therefore, considered more appropriate that they should hold the highest non-officer rank in the Royal Observer Corps.

(v) *Floor Supervisor.* It is suggested that the Floor Supervisor should hold the rank of Leading Observer. He will then have to exercise discipline over Plotters and will work under the Post Controller.

Pay

7. It is not possible to fix rates of pay for Chief Observers or Leading Observers employed in the Centre similar to those for Head Observer and Deputy Head Observer at Posts, because the conditions of service are dissimilar.

8. Except for the Duty Controller, R.O.C. Observers employed in Centre Crews have no administrative work outside their watching hours and their increased responsibilities and duties coincide with their watching hours. On the other hand, in the case of the Head Observer and Deputy Head Observer at the Post, their increased responsibilities occur outside watching hours, and when they are on watch as Observers their responsibilities are exactly the same as those of any other Observer on duty.

9. It is, therefore, suggested that in the case of the Chief Observer and Leading Observer (Class A and Class B) employed in the R.O.C. Centre, their higher rate of pay should be on an hourly basis as follows:

Chief Observer – 1/6d. per hour
Leading Observer – 1/4½d. per hour

10. Class "A" Chief and Leading Observers at Centres would continue to perform the same hours of duty demanded of other Class "A" Centre Observers. Comparative rates of pay according to the present proposals are shown in Appendix 'A' and the increased cost of this scheme is shown in Appendix 'B'.

(Sgd.) G.H. Ambler
Air Commodore
Commandant, Royal Observer Corps

ROC/S. 500/Org.
13th May, 1943.

Addendum A:

Proposed Rates of Pay (R.O.C. Centres)

Class 'A': Full-time Observers

	Observer	Leading Observer	Chief Observer
Per hour	1.3	1.4½	1.6
48 hours	3.0.0	3.6.0	3.12.0
Weekly Bonus	18.6	18.6	18.6
Total Weekly Pay	£3.18.6d	£4.4.6d	£4.10.6d

Class 'B':

	Observer	Leading Observer	Chief Observer
Per hour	1.3	1.4½	1.6.
24 hours	1.10.0	1.13.0	1.16.0
12 hours	15.0	16.6	18.0

Present Rates of Pay (R.O.C. Centres)

Duty Controllers (Class 'A', Full-Time):

Per hour	1.3
48 hours	3.0.0
Responsibility Pay	1.10.0
Weekly Bonus	18.6
Total	£5.8.6d

Note: The present higher pay for Duty Controllers as against the pay of the Head Observer provides a precedent for the proposal that Chief Observers in the Centre with direct operational responsibilities should be paid at a higher rate than the Head Observer.

Present Rates of Pay (R.O.C. Posts)

Class 'A', Full-Time Observers:

	Observer	*Leading Observer*	*Chief Observer*
Per hour (watching)	1.3	1.3	1.3
48 hours	3.0.0	48 hours watching not allowed	48 hours watching not allowed
44 hours	-	2.15.0	44 hours watching not allowed
32 hours	-	-	2.0.0
Responsibility Pay°	-	10.0	1.5.0
Weekly Bonus	18.6	18.6	18.6
Total Weekly Pay	£3.18.6d	£4.3.6d	£4.3.6d

Class 'B', Part-Time Observers:

	Observer	*Leading Observer*	*Chief Observer*
Per hour (watching)	1.3	1.3	1.3
24 hours (watching)	1.10.0	1.10.0	1.10.0
Responsibility Pay°	-	10.0	1.5.0
Total Weekly Pay	15.0	£1.5.0	£2.0.0

° Admin and Training

Addendum B:

INCREASED COST

Calculated on a basis of full-time (Class 'A') Observer

	£	s.	d.
3½ Post Controllers per Centre at 12/- per week increase	109.	4.	0.
3½ Assistant Duty Controllers per Centre at 12/- per week increase	109.	4.	0.
3½ Floor Supervisors per Centre at 6/- per week increase	54.	12.	0.
Cost per Centre	273.	0.	0.
39 Centres	£10,647		
4 R.O.C. Liaison Tellers per Sector at 12/- increase per week	124.	16.	0.
15 Affected Fighter Command Sectors	£1872.	0.	0.
Total increased cost	£12,519		

Memorandum No.5: Training of R.O.C. Centre Observers and Crews

Information.

1. No organised system for training Centre observers and crews exists at the present time, in consequence there is a wide variation in standards of efficiency throughout the Royal Observer Corps.

2. The work of plotters on R.O.C. Centres tables exactly corresponds with that performed by R.A.F. and W.A.A.F plotters on Filter-room tables; the high standard of qualifications required and the great care taken in selecting and training Filter-room personnel is well known and the requisite qualifications, selection and training for the equivalent R.O.C. duties should be no less exacting.

3. At present no system obtains for the selection and training of recruits. In most cases it has been the joint responsibility of Centre Controller and Duty Controllers. The practical training of a recruit has usually been delegated to any plotter considered capable. This casual system has proved very unsatisfactory.

4. It is not intended to press for all recruits to be sent for training to the Leighton Buzzard Training School as it is felt that a satisfactory compromise can be effected by appointing one woman at each R.O.C. Centre who, before her appointment, will attend and qualify at the School and will thereby be able to give instruction herself on R.A.F. lines: this technique and method is increasingly necessary for the R.O.C. to adopt.

5. At the same time it is considered essential to organise a scheme for giving progressive instruction to existing members and to make provision for such specialised instruction as it may be found necessary to introduce from time to time.

Proposal.

6. The proposals submitted require the institution and carrying out of a comprehensive scheme for the training of Centre observers: this will be treated in three parts:
   (i) Preliminary training of recruits.
   (ii) Specialised instruction for:
       (a) Duty Controllers
       (b) Centre Instructor (Woman)
   (iii) Normal progressive instruction of Centre observers and crews designed to follow a line parallel with that being undertaken for Post members.

7. To establish a minimum standard of efficiency both practical and theoretical which every Centre Observer shall be required to reach and to maintain.

8. To organise and carry out a compulsory test of every Centre observer at least once a year to ensure that he or she has attained and/or is maintaining the requisite minimum standard of efficiency.

9. To organise and carry out other optional graded tests for Centre observers.

Proposed organisation.

10. R.O.C. Headquarters. There is an officer at R.O.C. Headquarters responsible for the organisation of Centre training throughout the Royal Observer Corps.

11. Area Headquarters. The Operations Staff Officer at Area Headquarters will be responsible for all training within the Area.

12. Groups.
    (i) The Centre Controller will be directly responsible to the Group Commandant for all Centre training both elementary and normal.
    (ii) The Duty Controllers will be responsible to the Centre Controller for the normal training of their crews.
    (iii) The Centre Instructor (Woman) will undertake the preliminary selection of recruits to determine their suitability: she will then give instruction as directed by the Centre Controller.

13. Duties of Group Commandant and Centre Controller.
    (i) To see that the Duty Controllers are fitted to give the required instruction to their crews.
    (ii) To organise, set and correct tests.
    (iii) To see that the questions set are sent to the Area Staff Officer (para. 12) at least 7 clear days before the test is held.
    (iv) To see that opportunity is given to every observer to receive instruction and to take the Basic Test at least once a year.

14. Duties of Duty Controllers.
    (i) To take such tests as may from time to time be laid down by R.O.C. Headquarters.
    (ii) To attend such courses of instruction and to undertake such temporary duties away from their Centres as may be required from time to time by their Group Commandants.

15. Duties of Centre Instructor (Woman).
    (i) To attend and pass the W.A.A.F. Filterers' course at Leighton Buzzard.
    (ii) To attend any other course away from their Centre as required from time to time by her Group Commandant.

(iii)To select and give preliminary instruction to recruits. (See para. 18).

(iv)To give special instruction on the subjects taught at the W.A.A.F. course to any members sent to her for that purpose by the Centre Controller.

(v) To exercise a general supervision of the welfare of the women observers of the Centre and to advise the Group Commandant and Centre Controller on such matters when required.

16. Duties of Area Operations Staff Officers.

(i) To attend such courses of instruction as may be necessary from time to time and especially those to be held at the Psychology Laboratory, Cambridge, which are designed to fit them to apply and correct the tests for Duty Controllers.

(ii) To assist the Group Commandants and Centre Controllers in their Areas in all matters connected with training.

17. Instruction of Crews.

(i) The Duty Controller will be responsible to the Centre Controller for the training of his crew or crews; he may call on other members to deal with any parts of the necessary instruction if he considers they are better qualified than he is himself in that particular subject.

(ii) It is thought that all necessary training can easily be accomplished during normal watch hours; except during the summer it is rare for all hours of even one week to be fully occupied with operations.

(iii)This pre-supposes the permanent attachment of the Duty Controller to one or two definite crews; this is the general practice today throughout the Corps and its retention is considered most desirable.

18. Instruction of recruits.

(i) This is designed to fit a recruit to take his or hers place in a crew competent to perform *one* duty.

(ii) No attempt has been made beyond this to describe any course of instruction as it has been thought best to leave Instructors to their own methods.

19. Tests.
    (i) The scope of the present proposals is limited to the provision of a Basic Test.
    (ii) It is intended to proceed further and provide for an intermediate and a Master Test to form an exact parallel with the Post Training Scheme. (See paras. 21 and 22).
20. Basic Test.
This will be divided into six parts:
    (i) Ability to plot or tell at a rate of 10 plots per minute without ancillary information.
    (ii) Ability to fill at least two different positions in the Centre.
    (iii)Possession of a fair knowledge of Centre Procedure.
    (iv)Possession of an elementary knowledge of the History of the Royal Observer Corps.
    (v) Possession of an elementary knowledge of either:-
    (a) Post Procedure
    OR
    (b) The working of a Sector Operations Room.
    (vi)Possession of an elementary knowledge of and the ability to recognise from silhouettes and photographs 20 types of aircraft correctly from an episcope showing of 30 selected from those contained in the list for the Posts' Basic Test.

21.   Intermediate Test. It is provisionally intended that this shall be the same as that provided for the Posts' Basic Test plus the aircraft recognition contained in the Posts' Intermediate Test.
22.   Master Test. It is provisionally intended that this shall be the same as the Posts' Master Test, it will carry the right to the Spitfire badge. Neither of these last two tests may be passed by an observer until he or she has passed the previous Test.
23.   Increase of Personnel at Centres. The following increase of personnel is required to implement the scheme:
    (i) Centre Instructor (Woman). Apart from her training duties she will fill an increasing need of a Woman Welfare Officer brought about by the rising number of women observers in Royal Observer Corps Centres.

(ii) One Part-time Controller. (Or the equivalent), would raise the number of Duty Controllers from the present establishment of 3½ to a total of 4. It is considered that the increased mobility required of Duty Controllers for the purpose of attending Courses of Instruction (see paragraph 14), undertaking temporary duties with the R.A.F., etc., affords adequate justification for this small increase in establishment.

24. Rank of Centre Instructor. It is proposed to give the rank of Chief Observer (Woman) to the Centre Instructor.

(Sgd.) G.H. Ambler
Air Commodore
Commandant, Royal Observer Corps

ROC/S. 500/Org.
12th May, 1943.

Appendix VIII

Training

It is a curious fact that, prior to the Second World War, it was not one of the functions of the Observer Corps to recognize the different types of aircraft, but merely to report and "tell" everything that they saw or heard, irrespective of its type. There was, however, provision made in the procedure for distinguishing between bombers and fighters, regardless of nationality.

It was expected that all identification and filtering would be done in Royal Air Force Operations Rooms with the help of Radar. But it was soon realised that better use could be made of the Observer Corps, and that it was essential that not only should Observers be able to identify friend from foe, but also that recognition of different types was to become one of their most valuable qualifications.

Training was, therefore, at the commencement of war, on most elementary basis, and consisted in instruction in the use of the Post Instrument and in the reporting and telling of aircraft plots within sight or sound of the Post. The only issue made to Posts prior to the war for assistance in their duties was the book of British Silhouettes (A.P. 1480A). This issue was first made about four years before the war, and was maintained by means of the subsequent issue of all Amendment Lists. From September 1939 onwards, many additional publications were issued to Observer Posts showing silhouettes of German, Belgian, Dutch, Italian, French, and American Aircraft, but in November, 1940 it was decided to limit the issue of Recognition Publication to the following scale:

A.P. 1480A (British Aircraft)
A.P. 1480B (German Aircraft) One copy per Post and Centre
A.P. 1480C (Italian Aircraft)
A.P.1764 (Aircraft Recognition Wallet) Three copies for Post and Centre.

In addition to this the publications known as "Flight" and "The Aeroplane" proved invaluable for their sheets of photographic reproductions of aircraft of all types, and use was also made of Bakelite models of British and foreign aircraft, while in November 1940 Aeroplane Recognition Films were issued to Observer Group Officers with authority to show these by hire of projectors or of Cinema halls. In January, 1941 the Air Ministry was asked to provide an individual issue to all members of Parts 1, 2, 3, and 4 of "Aircraft Identification" published by "The Aeroplane", and also sets of Identification Playing Cards on a scale of two sets per Post and Centre. New transparencies showing British, German and Italian Aircraft were issued on a scale of 200 sets per Group, while each Post was authorised to purchase locally ten copies of each issue of the "Aeroplane Spotter".

The Corps was, of course, a voluntary civilian organisation and, naturally, the first effort to organise training came from certain enthusiasts who started the "Hearkers Club", in November 1939 on a local basis, and this Club expanded to 15 branches within the first twelve months. This club was an unofficial organisation within the Observer Corps, whose objects were to encourage members to improve their knowledge of aircraft recognition, and to provide a social contact between neighbouring Posts. Starting in the Southern area the Club spread rapidly; the various branches held monthly meetings at which lectures were given and competitions in aircraft recognition took place. Members were issued with Certificates of Proficiency on passing certain tests in aircraft recognition. The Club depended on subscriptions by its members for the purchase of lantern slides and instructional equipment and for other necessary expenses.

In February 1941, the Hearkers Club was merged into an official organization known as the Observer Corps Club, of which the organizing Secretary was a Mr. H. J. Lowings, one of the

Originators of the Hearkers Club. The aims of this new organization were:

(i) To increase the efficiency of members of the Observer Corps in the recognition of aircraft.
(ii) To provide for instruction and training in recognition, and to hold competition and tests.
(iii)To provide a means of social intercourse.

It was realised that the Club was doing very valuable work in raising the standard of recognition throughout the Corps, but it had become obvious that, if its activities were to be extended, some financial assistance would be required. The Commandant pointed out, in fact, that, in default of some such organization, the formation of an Observer Corps School would have to be considered, and this would prove a far more costly proposition. Treasury sanction was accordingly given, in February 1941, for a capital grant of £102 for the purchase of Lantern Slides for the Club, and an annual grant of £250 to supplement the Club's revenues. This sanction was obtained on the understanding that the annual grant should be reviewed in a year's time, in the light of the conditions then prevailing.

On the same terms the Treasury sanctioned the appointment of an additional part-time Assistant Observer Group Officer to undertake the duties of Organizing Secretary of the Club, including the giving of lectures on aircraft recognition, on the understanding that the officer concerned would be borne against one of the posts of that grade in the Southern Area. It was agreed that the officer concerned would be entitled to claim regulated travelling and subsistence expenses for journeys and absence on duty away from his normal station.

In April 1941, as a result of a Report rendered by the Committee on the Observer Corps to the Secretary of State for Air, on the status and conditions of service and personnel of the Observer Corps, certain decisions were reached by the latter; among those decisions it may be relevant to quote verbatim that paragraph dealing with "Training and Liaison with the Royal Air Force":- "In a Corps so widely dispersed and working in small detachments, it is impracticable to organize systematic training on the usual Service model for personnel who mostly work on a part-time basis and cannot all be assembled at the same time. Consequently, training must largely be organised locally by Head Observers under the guidance of the Observer Group Officers and their assistants. Valuable help in this direction has been given by an organization called "The Observer Corps Club" (previously known as the "Hearkers Club) and this club has now been given official recognition and a measure of financial support to enable it to widen its activities. Steps are also being taken to strengthen the Corps' liaison with the R.A.F. Units. The form and extent of training will be reviewed by the Air Ministry, Fighter Command and the Corps Commandant.

The first step towards the introduction of training, on an official basis, came with permission being granted by the Air Ministry for 40 officers or members of the Royal Observer Corps to be sent to the School of Aircraft Recognition in the Isle of Man. This permission was given in April 1941, the course being an Instructors' Course and lasting for a fortnight. This came as a result of the first meeting of a Sub-committee of the Synthetic Training Committee which had been formed to discuss the question of aircraft recognition training with regard to:

(i) Method of training to be adopted.
(ii) Style of material required for training and scales of issue.
(iii)Establishment of instructors.

At this meeting, which was held at the Air Ministry on April 15th, 1941, it was agreed that:

(a) Commands should be asked to do all they could to assist Royal Observer Corps personnel.
(b) Aircraft Identification Parts 1, 2 and 4 should be issued to the Royal Observer Corps.
(c) The question of reserving 40 vacancies at Ronaldsway, Isle of Man, for Royal Observer Corps personnel should be investigated.

During subsequent meetings of this Sub-Committee many points were discussed, and decisions taken regarding the supply of instructional apparatus, such as episcopes, silhouette transparencies, aircraft models and so on, and also matters affecting the method of instruction; in fact, a real effort was made to put training on a standardized and official basis.

It was found, however, by November, 1941, that both operations and training were being hampered by the difficulties experienced in obtaining from official sources up to date and suitable recognition material for all classes of personnel concerned in the Fighting and Civil Defence Services. An Inter-Service Recognition Committee was, therefore, formed to co-ordinate the other interests concerned, such as the Ministry of Home Security and the Ministry of Aircraft production, and the Commandant of the Royal Observer Corps was requested by the Air Ministry to appoint a representative to attend the meetings of this Committee. He accordingly nominated Air Commodore H. Le M, Brock, C.B., D.S.O., to attend as his representative.

Following the setting-up of this committee, every effort was made to speed up production of aircraft recognition training material, and the Ministry of Aircraft Production took special measures with this in view. Those measures were completed by May 1941, and from that date M.A.P. was responsible for the machinery for the production of nearly all forms of recognition material approved for official use. In a review of the Aircraft Recognition Problem (contained in a note by the Air Ministry I.S.R.C. 42(1)) which was considered by the Inter-Services Recognition Committee at their 10th meeting on January 2nd 1942, it appeared that despite the improvements that had been effected, the situation was unsatisfactory in that a high standard of visual recognition was not yet general throughout the Services. This appeared to be due to several causes, among which were lack of well-co-ordinated training between the services, lack of continued study and practice by personnel after their initial training, and delays in the production, issue and distribution of recognition training material. It was agreed at the meeting of the Inter Services Recognition Committee that Papers should be submitted by various departments and formations to cover the following main headings:

(i) Existing training methods.
(ii) Material used in existing training methods.
(iii) Proposals for improving training and co-ordination with other Services.

(iv) Shortcomings in existing material, and proposals for its improvement.

(v) Statements of difficulties experienced in obtaining material of the form and kind required.

As a result of a study of the paper submitted by the various Services concerned, it was decided to set up a Sub-Committee of the Inter Services Recognition Committee whose functions should be to co-ordinate training requirements and act as a clearing house for information on training methods. It should be a practical Committee and maintain the closest contact with the realities of the aircraft recognition problem. The membership of this Sub-Committee was agreed, and was to consist of representatives of the Admiralty, War Office, Air Ministry, D of I (S) (Air Ministry), Ministry of Aircraft Production, Royal Observer Corps and Ministry of Home Security. It was believed that the centralization of production of recognition material in the Ministry of Aircraft Production (which was agreed) would result in improvements both in its quality and quantity. In particular the work at the Ministry of Aircraft Production and that of the Sub-Committee on Recognition Training should remove the dangers which had accrued in the past through the use of unofficial recognition material.

Supply and distribution of aircraft recognition materials certainly improved from that date onwards, but it was not until the change of Commandant for the Royal Observer Corps took place, on June 25th 1942, that the actual training system commenced to be on an official and organized basis. Air Commodore Ambler, on July 6th, 1942 submitted a report on "The Royal Observer Corps Problems and some Recommendations", in which, among other points, he made various suggestions about training.

As he pointed out, training was at that time on a voluntary basis, and had been performed by the R.O.C. Clubs and, while he considered that the Clubs had carried out a very useful function, in his opinion training should become compulsory, and part of the official liabilities of the Royal Observer Corps Headquarters. He considered that pay, which had up to that time been only admissible for "A" and "B" members while actually on duty at

Post or Centre, should now be admissible for properly organized training periods and that travelling expenses and petrol allowances should be admissible to "A" and "B" members for this purpose. He recommended that training should be properly organised by the R.O.C. Headquarters, through Areas and Groups to Posts and Centres, and that training schedules should be prepared, the training at Post to be divided into two categories, Aircraft Recognition and Post Procedure, and at Centres into Plotting and Post Control. In his opinion, proficiency badges should be instituted, one for the attainment of an elementary and one for an advanced standard. This report was rendered in July 1942, and three months later on October 20th 1942, he submitted three Memoranda, of which Memorandum No.3 dealt in detail with the problem of training of R.O.C. Post Personnel.

On May 13th 1943, he submitted two further Memoranda, of which Memorandum No.5 had as its title "Training of R.O.C. Centre Observers and Crews.

Thus the whole system of training was put on a satisfactory system of organization and, from the system in force for the first three years of the war, which was voluntary and depending entirely on the goodwill and enthusiasm of Observers, it became the obligation of every member to ensure that he was adequately fitted for his task, while it was the responsibility of R.O.C. Headquarters to make certain that the necessary training was given and that the training materials were available.

A detailed description of the system of training in force in November 1944 is contained in Air Ministry Paper No.110, produced by the Air Ministry for the Select Committee on National Expenditure, Sub-Committee "D". This, which is an admirable summary of the method and system employed, may be given in full:

(i) Area Commandants are responsible, through their staff officers, for all training in their areas.

(ii) At Centres, preliminary training is given by the Woman Personnel Officer and selected Leading or Chief Observers. Practical training, during operations, is given under the general supervision of the Duty Controller on duty. There are no standard tests.

(iii) General supervision of the training of Post Observers is an important part of the duties of Group Officers, all of whom must have qualified at the R.A.F Central School of Aircraft Recognition. Under them, the actual instruction is given by Post Instructors (Chief Observers or Leading Observers) who must have passed the instructors' course and who are encouraged to attend a 7-day course for instructors at the R.A.F. School of Aircraft Recognition.

(iv) Post Instructors are required, as a condition of Service, to qualify for operational duties by passing a basic test and to re-qualify at intervals of six months. An Observer who is incapable of passing this test is regarded as being below operational standard and is discharged.

(v) Post Observers are encouraged to take higher tests, of which there are two:- an intermediate test and the master test. An Observer who has passed the master test can be regarded as an expert on aircraft recognition; he is entitled to wear a "Spitfire" Arm-badge.

(vi) Various devices are used in training, including model aircraft, Epidiascopes, 16mm cinematograph films and silhouette cards.

Addendum 1:

AIRCRAFT RECOGNITION MATERIAL

It seems generally agreed that there is today a certain lack of co-operation and standardisation of aircraft recognition material, leading to a profusion of efforts in some directions and a lack of adequate material in others.

Before suggesting certain general lines of approach, I take it that we must accept the position that there can be no official control of outside publishers in their efforts to popularise recognition material.

The people requiring recognition material are as follows:

The Services.
The Royal Observer Corps.

The Air Training Corps.
Roof Spotters, etc.

The main types of material available are:-
(1) Models (Bakelite etc., and full detailed types).
(2) Silhouettes (Air Ministry and "Aeroplane" are the only ones to be considered seriously).
(3) Photographs.
(4) Drawings: (a) Full chiaroscuro drawing; (b) Line drawings without shading (as in old version of A.P. 1480); (c) Detailed semi-sectional drawings (as published in "The Aeroplane").

Teaching experience, in the initial stages, seems to demonstrate the following points:
(1) That the question of size is of paramount importance. This applies particularly to photographs and models. If a learner is presented with a fairly large model (a Whitley, for example, of about 18" long), or photographs of the same size, the absorption of the characteristics of the aircraft is very quick in a reasonably quick mind.
(2) The complete failure of silhouettes *on their own* in these initial stages of instruction. The reason, I think, is that a silhouette, being like a blue print, needs reading, and it takes experience to fill out three-dimensionally what is purely a diagram. Silhouettes are, however, extremely valuable in the early stages to demonstrate the actual shapes, provided photographs are also provided. They are also very useful for comparison purposes.
(3) Small photographs are also inadequate, as it is very difficult to grasp essential shapes from such small presentation.
(4) A peculiar thing is noticeable after training on, say, two large photographs per type, combined with silhouettes. This is, that although the photographs only show two angles of the aircraft concerned (and if they were large and carefully chosen to illustrate the general structure of the plane) the learner is often quite able to recognise the plane from any angle when he sees it.
(5) The training which I believe is popular in certain places, which depends upon showing small and indistinct

photographs in order to familiarise learners with the distant appearance of aircraft, seems to me wrong in the early stages of instruction, and the same points as mentioned in (4) apply here, i.e. if the initial acquaintance with the plane is based upon two or three large photographs (together with demonstration of specific points on silhouettes) recognition is remarkably speeded up and a sure foundation laid.

(6) Failure to recognise aircraft in the air, and/or in photographic and other "trick tests" seems almost always to be traceable to lack of presentation of large images both in model, photographic or silhouette form, in the early stages: (No mention is made here of the obvious advantages of being shown the plane in reality).

(7) An extra point, if it may be laboured, concerning the essentiality of training on large images in the early stages.Most people react rather well to two specific approaches when being taught. The first approach is to grasp the general character of the plane with its obvious mental associations with everyday shapes, etc. Secondly, comes the careful analysis of individual parts. This second approach is quite impossible on small material. I cannot, of course, prove this, but time and time again it turns up in training.

(8) Following the learning of a reasonable number of standard types the value of comparative work is, I feel, very high. This particular aspect is best dealt with by silhouettes, but again they must be large.

(9) Another point of interest is the general demand for material to assist the progress from the unknown to the known in those who are already advanced in the subject, but who are confronted with unknown types. I have suggested below comparative wall charts, arranged on a classification by engines. (See D below). I would suggest the following types of material to be adopted as standard for all branches of the subject:

A. Models (as large as possible).

B. Large scale (double crown size) wall charts containing two large photographs, with three silhouettes printed smaller beneath. A specimen of this has been submitted.

C. The new version of the A.P. 1480, with silhouettes and view in juxtaposition. This would be for individual learning and records.

D. Comparative charts of silhouettes, based on classification of aircraft by engines. These could be produced ideally in wall chart form, and a specimen is attached. (The specimen is clearly inadequate, as it is a photographed copy of material used in A.P. 1480, and should be made from the original drawings, otherwise real sharpness cannot be obtained.)

E. Actual detailed photographs. There could be a "reference library" of these in each training centre or recognition room.

F. Miscellaneous test material of all kinds, distant views, technical details, "track shots", "dark glasses tests", and other ingenious devices which have been suggested from time to time.

C.H. GIBBS-SMITH,
Photograph Division, Ministry of Information; Royal Observer Corps.
Lecturer on Aircraft Recognition to 702 Squadron, A.T.C.

Addendum 2:

"THE OBSERVER POST – LAYOUT, AND PERFORMANCE OF PERSONNEL"
Operational Research Section Report No. 672 (Appendix "B")

THE POST
1. *Siting.* Requirements are:
    (i)   Good field of view;
    (ii) Good hearing conditions;
    (iii) Accessibility.
    A good field of view is of limited value if hearing is bad. Posts in towns and on buildings tend to be inferior to those in the country because of outside noise; nearby railways, aerodromes and main roads are undesirable. Good sites tend to be on an elevation in the middle of an open valley or on the top of a hill. Post siting is a skilled and important job,

195

requiring considerable experience of conditions at variously sited, existing Posts; a site is best chosen by a study of a contoured map, confirmed by reconnaissance of likely sites. One well-sited Post may be worth two badly-sited; a considerable proportion of existing R.O.C. Posts still remain for which the cost of resisting would soon be repaid by the increased return in value for the cost of maintaining the Observers on duty.

2. *The Post Building.* The Post Building is required:
   (i)   to give shelter to the Observers,
   (ii) to provide a good outlook point,
   (iii) to provide a good hearing place.

   A snug and compact watch compartment is best, both for keeping warm and for hearing aircraft noise. To obtain a good outlook may call for a high Post Building, and this often entails wind noise which seriously masks aircraft sound. Such Posts should be fitted with coir-matting windscreens, which materially reduce wind noise. A "Tumulus" Post (a watch compartment at ground level, well banked around with earth, so as to produce a smooth flow of wind over the Post) is probably best at sites where it affords an adequate view, because it gives optimum hearing conditions. In many existing Posts, the shelter from stray noise provided by the "cubby hole" enables aircraft to be heard clearly there when they are inaudible at the outlook point.

CAPABILITIES OF OBSERVERS

3. *Observers.* A crew of two at a Post fits well; three is a crowd, and a single observer cannot maintain continuous vigilance (and may be lonely). With two Observers, for much of the time one man is alert and the other relaxes; at busy periods one observes while the other wears the telephone. Further investigation of the best method of keeping watch (length of period of alertness, and methods of visual scan) is desirable; much relevant information concerning naval look-outs is available from Admiralty and Coastal Command experience. During a period of six months recently, 1183 "visual" Post reports, covering 46 Posts reports, covering 46 Posts in 9

Groups, were analysed. In 1130 reports, type was stated definitely; 27 reports said "plane" (i.e. type unrecognized) and 26 defaulted in any reference to type.

4. Observers should be free from hearing defects, and have 6/6 vision for distant objects. A temperament suited to long periods of waiting and keeping watch is needed; typically, a placid middle age temperament. Apart from this, age (and sex) appears to be relatively immaterial.

RECOGNITION

5. *Recognition*. Visual aircraft recognition is exceedingly good, Type and sometimes also Mark of aircraft, or special markings being recognised. Normally an Observer recognises all aircraft he sees almost at once, sometimes using binoculars for those more distant or to confirm direct inspection; the skill and quality of an Observer is displayed in absence of hesitation and delay in deciding on his recognition. Visual recognition has been the subject of much attention, both in official training and in study arising from voluntary keenness; education by overhearing (and criticising) the recognitions given by brother Posts is probably an equally potent factor in producing good recognition. It is believed to take 6 months or so before an Observer is fully adept at recognition.

6. Sound recognition is also quite good; especially, Observers know the sound of the flying usual in their vicinity, recognising both the type of aircraft and the activity on which it is engaged, and can eliminate from their reports these local flying aircraft if not wanted by Centre. Aside from common types of activity, the readiness and confidence with which Observers give type by sound varies very much from one Observer Group to another; in some, type is given as a matter of course, in others, Observers will hardly venture an opinion as to type. This variation appears to correspond to real differences between Groups in ability to recognise type by sound. Further investigation is wanted into the process and conditions of sound-recognition; the matter is not simple, and almost certainly depends on the Observer being thoroughly familiar with his surroundings. In particular,

Observers and Centre Plotters should be helped by information as to which aircraft types sound similar; e.g. Lancaster and Mosquito (some close resemblances are unexpected). The practical importance of sound recognition is shewn by the very widespread spontaneous pressure on Observers by centre Plotters asking "What do you think it sounds like?" Centre quite often urgently needs this information to sort out the Posts' reports of aircraft to form connected tracks. Certain Observers have reached the stage of giving sound recognition spontaneously.

7. Observers generally are very good at initiating a report about any aircraft which sounds either suspicious or in trouble. The reliability of such reports is good; in case of doubt, Posts tend to the side of making a report rather than to silence.

POST REPORTING: VISUAL

8. *Post Reporting: Visual.* Posts report the position of seen aircraft as a grid reference (using a unit square of 2 KM. side). This is done either by estimating by eye the height of the aircraft, setting this on the height bar of the Post Instrument and pointing the Instrument at the aircraft, so bringing the Instrument-pointer over the appropriate square on the map; or by direct judgement of the grid-reference without troubling to use the Instrument. In practice, both methods are usually quite accurate (that is, errors are not larger than the distance an aircraft moves in the time taken to make a report, or the uncertainty introduced in plotting at Centre); this accuracy is believed to depend on the fact that the Observer quite often overhears plots on the same aircraft from brother-Posts and notices (and afterwards avoids) errors in his own plotting. Although experienced Observers can, when busy, perfectly well dispense with using the Instrument, it is essential for achieving and maintaining accuracy that the Instrument be used and that Posts periodically check their own estimates of height by means of a cross-bearing overhead from a brother-Post.

9. Posts in North-Western Area report position of seen aircraft by giving a bearing (in clock minutes) and a distance (in

miles), instead of by giving a grid reference. This method is here recommended because it is the more natural form for a Post report (it separates the direct reading, bearing which should be very accurate, from the Observer's estimate, distance); because it encourages Posts to obtain "corrected" heights (they need encouragement) if they hear directly bearing given by their brother-Post, instead of having to reconvert a grid reference to a line of bearing (this process of reconversion introduces an uncertainty which can make a "corrected" height decidedly incorrect); because it brings "visual" and "heard" procedure into line; and because, from a Post Instrument of reasonable design, bearing and range can be more easily read than can a grid-reference. Experiments have shown that, as regards accuracy and speed of Centre plotting, there is little to choose between the two systems.

10. Post Observers' estimates of height are believed, on very scanty precise data, to contain an average error of about 10%; there is a tendency which was very marked early in the war, but is to a considerable degree eradicated now that high-flying aircraft are less rare, to underestimate markedly the height of aircraft above about 15,000 ft.

POST REPORTING: SOUND

11. *Post Reporting: Sound.* Posts are now instructed to report the location of aircraft heard, giving the bearing of the sound (in clock minutes), the direction of flight of the aircraft, and the angle of elevation of the sound (quoted in units of thousands of feet of height at a distance of 5 miles). Many Observers also give on request their estimate of the actual height of the aircraft; a few Observers sometimes give this spontaneously.

12. Exact data on the accuracy of Observers' reports on sound are very scanty; more would be valuable both for the immediate bearing on the methods of working of Ground Observers and for general scientific information as to the capability of trained human hearing. The confidence in, and almost certainly the average accuracy of, sound reporting varies greatly between Observer Groups, and between Posts in a Group; in addition to personal differences between individual Observers.

13. It is generally understood that Observers are supposed to report the direction of the sound as they hear it, that is, without making any allowance for the fact that the real direction of the aircraft at any time is ahead of its sound. Such evidence as is available, however, suggests that when "pointing at sound", Observers unconsciously allow, in part at least, for the sound lag.

14. Accuracy of bearings appears to be generally as good as is required for Centre plotting; that is to say, errors appear rarely to exceed two or three "clock" minutes, and a similar uncertainty is introduced by the variable time taken to make and receive a Post report, in which time the aircraft moves. It is not clear how far errors in reported bearings are due to the Observer's error in locating sound and how far to errors in reading the Instrument, which has no well-defined index marking the bearing reading. The Observer may be in doubt as to the direction of faint, distant sounds, but this appears not to be of great practical seriousness. Observers appear also to give satisfactorily the direction of flight, and rarely say "no direction".

15. Reasons of practical importance make especially serious the dearth of definite information on the accuracy with which Observers judge the angle of elevation of sound, or the actual height of an aircraft; it is not even clear on what physical factors Observers base their judgement, how far success may depend on familiarity with the particular type of aircraft, and within what bounds success may be expected; there are indications that judgements of angle of elevation and of estimated height are mutually consistent, and that Observers who are good at one are also good at the other. It seems that many Posts can give both angles of elevation and direct estimated height with a degree of accuracy of definite practical value.

POST REPORTING: OVERHEAD

16. *Post Reporting: "Overhead"*. There is a widespread belief that a report of "Overhead" at a Post is more accurate than a grid-reference; especially, Posts like to obtain "corrected" heights on an "overhead" report from a brother Post. In practice,

"overhead" reports prove to be decidedly less accurate than grid references, especially on high-flying aircraft. Posts usually anticipate when saying "overhead now."

THE POST INSTRUMENT

17. The whole job of the Observer would be done better if the Post Instrument were redesigned so that it could be sighted and read with less effort and more comfortably (more convenient lay out and controls, clearer scales, no need to stoop, etc.).

18. The Instrument should embody a monocular or binoculars; the best choice of balance between the rival claims of magnification and field of view requires investigation, having regard to the optimum type of binoculars to be provided also for No. 2 at the Post, to day and night conditions, and to prevailing visibility. The telescope in the Instrument is wanted primarily for careful inspection and recognition of aircraft, particularly at considerable distances (since the Instrument affords a steady support, the magnification can be greater than with hand-held glasses) and for following out, to greater distances or in twilight, targets fading from the unaided eye.

RECOMMENDATIONS

19. *Summary of Recommendations for the Existing System.*

   (i)   A considerable number of badly-sited Posts should be re-sited (para. 1).

   (ii) Coir-matting windscreens should be fitted to many Posts to reduce wind-noise. (para. 2).

   (iii) Post Observers should have at least normal vision and hearing (para. 4).

   (iv) Observers should be given elementary instruction in best methods of eye-scan, and the importance of scanning should be stressed (para. 3).

   (v)   Study of recognition should not be confined to visual recognition, it should deal also with the other aspects which are utilised at Post particularly recognition potentialities by sound, as well as by speed and behaviour (para.6).

(vi) The Post Instrument should be completely re-designed. The necessary experience to make a good job of this is believed to be possessed by the Cambridge Psychological Laboratory and by A.D.R.D.E. (paras. 17-18).

(vii) Posts should report to Centre the positions of seen aircraft by giving bearings and distance from the post, rather than by giving grid-reference (para.7).

(viii) Posts should not report aircraft as "overhead" (para. 16.).

Appendix IX

Recruitment and Manpower

The whole problem of recruitment and manpower for the Royal Observer Corps was one which was always fraught with difficulties which were inherent in the very system itself. The terms and conditions of service at the outbreak of the Second World War have already been given in detail in Section V of the Narrative, and these terms continued, subject to changes in pay and status, throughout the war.

Although a considerable economy in manpower was effected through a combination of the services of part-time and whole-time members, this brought with it corresponding disadvantages. Part-time members, though their services were valuable, could not in all cases be of equal value with those working full-time and, in any case, problems of establishments and manning were inevitably created. It must be remembered too, that, in contrast with the civil defence forces generally, there were no lengthy stand-by periods. It was necessary for Observers at the Posts to be constantly on the look-out, and similarly the Plotters in the Centres had to remain always alert in order that anything observed at a Post might be made known to the Air Defences or to the Flying Control organisation within the shortest possible space of time.

As the attendance in hours of part-time members varied between individuals and even for each individual from time to time, it was not possible to fix establishments in terms of persons, and they were accordingly fixed in terms of man-hours per week. Group Commandants then decided in the light of local conditions, the number of persons required to produce the requisite output of man-hours. Normally no part-time members worked less than 12 hours a week, and no full-time member less than 48 hours.

The recruitment of full-time Observers was through the Ministry of Labour and National Service, and vacancies in officer ranks were filled by the promotion of Observers. Under the R.O.C. (Employment) Order, 1941 and 1942, made by the Air Council under Defence Regulation 29B, members of the R.O.C. were required to continue in their employment unless released. Under the same Regulation a member of the R.O.C. could be declared by the Commandant to be mobile, subject to the right of appeal. This power was obtained in connection with the Seaborne scheme, but was not, in fact, put into operation, as a number of volunteers was more than adequate.

By the third year of the war, it had become evident that changes in organisation, and in terms of recruitment and in discipline generally were necessary in order to produce the maximum state of efficiency possible. With the introduction of a serving officer of the Royal Air Force as Commandant of the R.O.C. in 1942 closer touch was obtained between the two Services and a more practical organization was formed. In a report on R.O.C. problems which the Commandant submitted in July 1942, he emphasized the point that the problem of manning the Posts was absolutely separate and distinct from that of manning Centres. He believed that the former was really a man's job, but that a relatively older man, provided that his sight and hearing were not impaired, could be efficient at a Post when he would not be efficient at a Centre. On the other hand he considered that, the character of the work in the Centre, though exactly the same as that in any type of Fighter Operation Room, was even more onerous and demanded a higher standard of operative. As a result of visits to some 17 R.O.C. Centres, he found that the consensus of opinion of the Controllers was that the maximum average age of men efficient in that type of work was from 40 to 45 years of age, while for woman the maximum age was some 10 years lower. In any case a leavening of youth was desirable. Those of the Class 'B' men left in industry were having to work longer hours in their civilian occupation and thus had less time and energy for R.O.C. work.

The Commandant recommended that young women should be employed in the Centre, and that the same type should be called upon for this work as were being employed in the W.A.A.F. as Clerks-Special Duties. He considered that there should be little difficulty in obtaining girls who could still live in their own homes, as the Centres were in populated districts.

As a result of these recommendations, which eventually, in effect, resolved themselves into a proposal to replace some 1,400 men of over 50 years of age (of whom 200 were full-time and the remainder part-time) by 700 immobile women under 35 years of age, it became necessary for the Parliamentary Under-Secretary of State for Air to make a statement in the House of Commons on November 25th 1942. He defended the proposals and combated the rather wide-spread misconception that it was intended to make wholesale dismissals in the R.O.C. It may be mentioned that, of the 1,400 persons concerned there were 25 over 70 years of age, 200 between 61 and 70, and the balance between 51 and 60, while the top age limit in Fighter Command Operations Rooms for work in similar kind was 35 years of age.

In the meantime, it was becoming increasingly evident that the original purpose and function of the R.O.C. were being swamped by the additional duties that had been added since the beginning of the war and operationally the Corps was under strength. The Ministry of Labour agreed accordingly to do all in their power to supply the R.O.C. with 1,400 full-time women, of whom 840 were now to replace the 1,400 (mainly part-time) older men, while 560 were required to bring the strength of the crews up to operational requirements.

By May 1943, after 6 months intensive effort by the Ministry only the approximate equivalent of 700 full-time women had been recruited into the R.O.C. and the flow was showing distinct signs of decreasing. Those recruited had proved an unqualified success and justified the policy adopted. The supply was unfortunately shortest in those places where the operational need was greatest, namely in the R.O.C. Centres serving No.11 Group R.A.F. and to some extent, No.10 Group, R.A.F. Not only that, but the demands for additional personnel when the Decentralized Air Raid Warning Scheme came into effect, in August 1943, would become urgent in those very areas.

The proposal was made, therefore, by the A.O.C.-in-C., Fighter Command that a certain number of W.A.A.F. should be attached to the R.O.C.; this would also have the advantage of giving to those selected experience in R.O.C. work, bringing the R.A.F. into closer contact with the R.O.C. side of the Raid Reporting Organisation, with advantages to both the R.A.F. and the R.O.C.

This proposal was not viewed with favour by Air Ministry authorities at a very high level, and an alternative scheme adopted, by which girls in the 1918/23 class who opted for the W.A.A.F were allowed to join the R.O.C. on deferred service, had produced only a very meagre supply, as was explained at a meeting at the Ministry of Home Security on September 22nd 1943. In fact, only 115 women out of 2039 interviewed during the first ten weeks of the scheme chose to join the R.O.C. on those terms. This was not altogether surprising, as Treasury authority was not obtainable for the grant of lodging allowance for girls appointed to Centres outside living distance of their homes.

There were by this time four schemes of recruitment for women observers in being:

(i)   The normal intake of immobile women under 35.
(ii) The deferred W.A.A.F Scheme.
(iii) A scheme launched by the Association of Girls' Training Corps.
(iv) A campaign backed by publicity for the recruitment of girls under 18¼ years of age.

It was now agreed that 460 W.A.A.F might be employed on a purely temporary basis on the understanding that efforts to replace these by civilians were to be unabated. For the remainder of the war W.A.A.F were employed in R.O.C. Operation Rooms as the supply of personnel continued to be a problem of continual difficulty.

To sum up, it would appear that the problem of supply of personnel for a service of this type will always be one of major difficulty. In order to keep enthusiasm at a reasonably high pitch during peace it is essential to stress the social and 'Club' side, and in this lies one of its greatest assets, the bringing together of men and women from all ranks of life and from all trades and professions. The natural leaders will tend, on all occasions, to come to the fore, and, if training performed on a satisfactory basis and they are in consequence qualified for that leadership, the general tone and feeling will be admirable. In time of war, it proved essential to modify this 'Club' side and Air Commodore Ambler's re-organisation, though it appeared ruthless to some, was of vital necessity to the well-being of the Royal Observer Corps. Though considerable dissatisfaction was aroused throughout the Corps by his elimination of those over 50 years of age at Centres, there were many who realised that this move was necessary. The re-actions of men of that age, in a large number of cases, were not sufficiently quick and certain to deal with the ever-growing complexity of modern operations.

On the other hand, the conflicting claims of other forms of service are bound to present a problem to those responsible for the allocation of personnel among the defences and in industry. It is doubtful whether, should the occasion rise again, it will be possible to rely to such an extent on the voluntary spirit, and whether it may not be necessary to ensure that those in industry are not paid on a higher level than those in a service of this nature. Provided however, that the peace-time training and Esprit de Corps are maintained there will always be a trained nucleus on which to rely should war break out once more, and there will always be, undoubtedly, a large number of men and women who will be ready to form part of that nucleus.

Addendum:

ROYAL OBSERVER CORPS CENTRES – MEN OVER 50
Statement by the Parliamentary Under-Secretary of State for Air
on the Motion for the Adjournment

House of Commons – November 25th, 1942

I am grateful to the Hon. and gallant Member for South Cardiff (Colonel Evans) for giving an opportunity of raising this matter on the Adjournment, and I apologise to other Hon. Members who may have wished to speak. I am sure that they will appreciate that time is limited, and I am glad that we have this opportunity, because I hope to be able to clear up some misconceptions. There is no question of wholesale dismissals in the Royal Observer Corps.

The change we are now proposing is due to altered operational requirements and the extended operational duties of the Royal Observer Corps. It affects approximately 1400 personnel out of the total strength of the Corps. There have been many unwitting misrepresentations in the Press as to the effect of this order. It has been represented that it is a reflection on the good work which the Royal Observer Corps have done. There is no question that the Royal Observer Corps members have fulfilled patriotically their part in the air defence of this country, but new methods and new equipment must be operated to the maximum efficiency, and to this end the order for the gradual replacement of the over fifties and the substitution of them by immobile women is introduced in order to increase the efficiency of plotting and telling.

The Royal Observer Corps plays a vital role in air defence. It is the ears and eyes of the Royal Air Force. It plots and it tracks all the aircraft, both friendly and hostile. This is necessary from the operational standpoint, particularly at night, otherwise it is impossible to separate the tracks of friendly and hostile aircraft. It will interest the House to know that the vast increase in night operational flying and in other types of night flying, including night instruction, over the last two years have made the work in these observation centres to-day approximately of the same pressure and volume as was met with during the relatively short time of the blitzes when the air force of the enemy was at its greatest against this country in 1940-1941.

There is a constant and ever-increasing pressure going on in these centres. It will interest the House again to know that the Royal Observer Corps has guided, in conjunction with other methods, an average of about 20 bombers a month to safety, and the figure was about 40 last month. But the figure should be higher. It has to be higher if we are to get the maximum safety among all these bombers which are returning from offensive operations over Germany. When I said the result should be better still the House will be with me when I say that we should be ruthless in our determination to introduce methods to get the highest efficiency in this service, irrespective of personal considerations.

The order does not affect men on posts, many of whom are over 50, who can still efficiently carry out their work, very often in exceedingly difficult conditions in posts, it only affects men at centres engaged in this plotting and telling. The work on which they are engaged corresponds almost exactly to the work carried on in Fighter Command operations rooms. As my Hon. and gallant friend and Member for North St. Pancras (Wing Commander Grant-Ferris) said, we are having in our Fighter Command operations rooms to reduce our top age. The work is of a novel sort and requires young, active brains to adapt themselves to it.

There is an old cry, 'Too old at 50', which may apply to some things which may not apply to others, but it certainly does apply to this particular type of work, which imposes a constant strain which, as we have found by experience young people can stand the best. Some Hon. Members over 50 – I am not quite there myself – still work competently and efficiently in various walks of life, but how many over 50 could suddenly learn all there is to know about the conversion of sound circle heights into corrected heights, involving angle distance plotting and a new method evolved by scientists working directly for the Royal Observer Corps, and the accurate computation of range and angle by plotters, all in a matter of seconds? After all, Fighter Command is responsible for the safety of this country from air attack and has found it necessary to impost a top limit, for this work, of 35. We have had anxiety from the last 18 months as to the work carried on at these centres, and now that new and complicated apparatus which I know the House would not expect me to enlarge upon here to-day is being introduced for operation by the Royal Observer Corps, quite frankly we are worried as to whether our top age limit of 50 will give us the required efficiency. Indeed, the time may come, as pressure on the R.O.C. centres becomes greater and more scientific apparatus is produced, when we may have to go below 50.

These centres contain people of a fairly high average age, as many of the younger men of the Royal Observer Corps have gone to the Forces. Of the 1,400 persons engaged we have 25 over 70, 280 between 61 and 70 and the balance of about 1,400 are between 51 and 60. The Hon. Gentlemen the Member for Ipswich (Mr.

Stockes) used the argument that he had men over 50 who were splendid men and who could do this work. I would not deny that in exceptional cases men over 50 can do this work, but you cannot introduce a system to check the individual efficiency of each man. After all, the yardstick of age is what we have accepted in our public and industrial life as being broadly the measure by which we say whether a man shall or shall not continue his work. There are always exceptions, but so much above the Fighter Command age limit is our top limit of 50 that I do not think it would be possible to legislate for exceptional cases. We must accept the yardstick of age. My Hon. and gallant Friend the Member for South Cardiff asked about the man-power position. Well, the men displaced will be given the opportunity or transferring to Royal Observer Corps posts in the neighbourhood. Their work will be in exposed places and not so pleasant, but already there are men of 50 doing this work gallantly, and I see no reason why they should not be able to do this work well. We shall transfer them to vacancies where we can, and the balance will be available for other war work.

Of the 1,400 men, some 200 are full-time and the remainder are part-time. These 1,400 men will be replaced by 700 immobile women under 35. These men will be given the opportunity of working at the posts, and the remainder, I am quite sure, will be glad to do their part in the war effort by fire-watching or doing some other national work in which their services will be useful. I submit it would be better to have those 1,200 men, or such proportion as we cannot absorb at the posts, on fire-watching or some form of war work, who are not particularly suitable for this work at the Centres, as we have found by experience, and let them do that work for which they are suitable. I submit that the resistance to this order and the protests are largely based on misapprehensions. The order is not unpopular in large sections of the Royal Observer Corps itself. We have had complaints from posts in several places in the country as to the slow working at the Centres.

We hope now to make the functioning of these Centres so efficient as to ensure their continuation as a vital part of our air defence able to absorb this new technique and these new appliances, able to adapt themselves to these new methods and to the increased work as these are met with. We save man-power, we use women where men have previously been used, and we release these men for other forms of work for which they are more suitable than they are for that on which we have employed them in the past; but more than that – what I am sure the House will accept from me as being the most cogent argument of the lot – we have a greater chance of saving the lives of our airmen by increasing the efficiency of our air defence system.

Appendix X

The Human Element

There is no doubt whatever that the Royal Observer Corps presented, for those whose responsibility consisted in the supply of manpower, one of the most difficult problems of the war. Owing to the policy by which it was decided to preserve the voluntary system in manning this body, and also to maintain the civilian organisation and to avoid any idea of militarisation, it was difficult for those in authority to produce argument in favour of giving preference to the Corps in the supply of personnel.

It is, in fact, an amazing thing that the Royal Observer Corps was manned by such an efficient body of men, when the anomalous condition under which their work was performed are considered. Naturally those conditions gave rise on many occasions, to complaints by members, more especially on the policy of non-militarisation had rendered the disciplinary attitude of the Corps more a matter for each individual's conscience than is generally the case in a more regular form of Service.

The conditions under which the type of men lived that formed the major part of the Royal Observer Corps were, in fact, carried forward from their pre-war existence into their full or part-time war occupation; and, in many cases they were indeed still performing their peace time occupations in parallel with their work with the Corps. Thus it was, to some extent, necessary in this, as in other forms of part-time service, to adopt a more individual form of disciplinary code than was the case in a full-time uniformed service.

This attitude of relying on the individual conscience was satisfactory at the commencement of the war, but with the passing of the months and years, and as the strain increased, both mentally and physically, it became obvious that the existing conditions were not producing the best results; Esprit de Corps needed to be stimulated by the removal of tired, inefficient or dissentient members, and by the introduction of young blood into the system. A disciplinary standard was required even though it was considered essential to avoid full militarisation, and this was achieved, at the cost of some heart-burnings, by the compulsory wearing of uniform and by the introduction of rank gradings into the Corps. These measures, together with the employment of young women and the elimination of the men over 50 years of age, provided the necessary stimulus, and introduced a revitalizing element into the Royal Observer Corps, the results of which were immediately apparent and of considerable value in the efficient functioning of the Corps.

Owing to the extraordinary diversity of occupations from which the members of the Corps were drawn, owing to the scattered spacing of posts and centres and, not least, owing to the varied grades of society to which the members belonged, the problem of smooth organisation of this body of men was one of no little interest and of considerable complexity.

It is, in fact, a notable tribute to the democratic principles of this very involved society of modern times that the Royal Observer Corps carried out its duties with so few rifts within the lute. If one considers any one of the Areas, for instance the Midland Area, it will be found that members were drawn from a hundred and one different occupations. Extending from the Scottish border, down the line of the Pennine Chain, covering the broad Ridings of Yorkshire, the Lincolnshire Fens, the manufacturing cities of the Midlands, the great wool towns of Yorkshire, and the North Sea ports and fishing villages, this Area gives a comprehensive picture of varying occupations from which the Observers were drawn. Labourer, squire, gamekeeper, parson, wool operative, clerk, fisherman and many another type furnished the bulk of the watchers at Posts and the crews at Centres, and, be it said to their credit, men were not ashamed to work under those who in private life were in their employ.

The welding together of these scattered units and individuals into a cohesive working organisation was the task of those much-travelled men, the observer group officers, and their work cannot be under-estimated. The majority were fortunately gifted with tact, energy and enthusiasm, were this not so they would not have met with the success which they undoubtedly achieved. That, in fact, was the domestic responsibility of the Corps and its officers, but the task which set those responsible for it a major problem was the actual supply of personnel for the Post and Centres.

As the war progressed, and the demands for manpower for every Service increased, those members of the Corps who were fit for active service and who were doing part-time service with the Royal Observer Corps began to be de-reserved from their civilian occupation. In other words, the more youthful members, those best fitted for that reason for the quick decisions necessitated by their work, began to be withdrawn and called up for the fighting Services, and a dangerous shortage of the right type of observer became apparent.

That was the point at which appeared the flaw in the policy that had been adopted towards the Corps. Had it been, from the start, recognised as one of the most important elements in the Air Defence of Great Britain, a uniformed, disciplined Corps, well-known, to the public generally, and in particular to those responsible for assessing the relative priorities of the various branches of war work, the dangerous situation that now arose might never have eventuated. As a fact, however, the result of this dangerous shortage was the introduction of women into the Corps, a measure which, though suggested prior to the war, might never otherwise have been adopted.

As has been said, this innovation was an unqualified success. There were a small number of women employed at Observer Posts, but the majority were found to be admirably suited for work in the operations rooms in the Observer Centres; the suitability of women for this type of occupation had, of course, been recognised by the Royal Air Force within the first few weeks of war. But war-time industry and the women's branches of the fighting Services were also making their demands on the supply of female personnel, and there never proved to be an adequate supply of women available to meet the demands of the Royal Observer Corps. The result of this was the temporary employment of W.A.A.F. in some numbers to fill the vacancies in the Observer Corps operations rooms. This measure, though meeting with considerable opposition; proved to have its corresponding advantage, in that it had the effect of familiarising the W.A.A.F. who were employed in this way with the work being done by their 'opposite numbers' in the Royal Observer Corps.

As a result of the experience gained during the war, and in considering the future of the Royal Observer Corps in the light of that experience, it is possible to suggest with some degree of accuracy the type of person needed for this work and the method in which they should be employed. There is a sharp dividing line between the personality and character of the operator in an operation room and the observer suited for work at Posts. The former needs to have a good standard of education, because the problems of a modern operation room are highly complex, and needs also to be quick and accurate, as inaccuracy in plotting or in telling may have disastrous consequences. Above all, perhaps, it is necessary to be gregarious, as without that quality the strain of the work might, at times, prove intolerable.

For the worker on an Observer Post a slower mentality can be tolerated, but what is essential is the capacity to endure loneliness and the extremes of weather; perhaps the best example of a suitable type is the gamekeeper, shepherd or countrymen generally, as an Observer must have an eye for country and an accurate knowledge of the locality in which his post is situated.

It is suggested that if operations rooms are largely staffed by women, which is the obvious trend, and as the work in all operations rooms is very similar, personnel should be interchangeable between the Royal Air Force and the Royal Observer Corps in this capacity. What is principally necessary, if the Corps is still required as a peacetime organisation, is the maintenance of that esprit-de-corps which was engendered during the years of war. With the natural reaction which inevitably sets in at the conclusion of a major conflict, more than the original enthusiasm will be needed to man a Corps for the members of which active service should not reasonably be anticipated within the near future. Something on the lines of a regular formation, uniformed, disciplined, well-advertised, and reasonably paid, even if this pay is only in the nature of a retaining fee.

With these advantages, and with the traditions evolved during the years of war, there is little doubt that the Royal Observer Corps will go from strength to strength.